The Promise of Narrative Change: Living the Why to Thrive

Carson O. Mouser

Parson's Porch Books

The Promise of Narrative Change: Living the Why to Thrive

ISBN: Softcover 978-1-951472-18-4

Copyright © 2016 by Carson O. Mouser

All rights reserved. No part of this book may be reproduced or transmitted in any form or by any means, electronic or mechanical, including photocopying, recording, or by any information storage and retrieval system, without permission in writing from the publisher.

To order additional copies of this book, contact:

Parson's Porch Books
1-423-475-7308
www.parsonsporch.com

Parson's Porch Books is an imprint of Parson's Porch & Company (PP&C) in Cleveland, Tennessee. PP&C is an innovative company which raises money by publishing books of noted authors, representing all genres. All donations from contributors and profits from publishing are shared with the poor.

The Promise of Narrative Change:

Living the Why to Thrive

Dedication

For Tina, my wife and my best friend, whose love makes joyous and radiant the path we walk hand in hand.

Table of Contents

Introduction	9
Chapter 1	13
Change and Transition: Two Sides of the Same Coin	
Chapter 2	24
The Forest of Change and Transition	
Chapter 3	28
The Usual Guides through the Forest	
Chapter 4	35
Reclaiming Story-telling for Change and Transition	
Chapter 5	47
Weaving Narratives for New Life	
Chapter 6	53
The Practical Example	
Chapter 7	104
New Life Begins: Living Why to Thrive	
Appendix 1	107
Appendix 2	120
About the Author	145
End Notes	149
Select Bibliography	152

Introduction

The aroma of dark roasted coffee, porcelain cups clattering against saucers, the steam blowing from the espresso machine blanketed the whispered conversations of couples, threesomes, and foursomes sitting around tables scattered around the coffee shop miming a living room. The heat from the hot coffee warmed my hands as I brought the cup to my lips.

"Hey," my friend Tim said, "You're an orphan."

"What?" I said, spilling a drop of coffee on the saucer. "What did you say?"

"You're an orphan. Both of your parents have died."

"Oh," I said.

Until that moment I had not thought about myself that way. After that moment, the only thing I could think about was what it meant to be an orphan. I was no longer somebody's son. I was no longer a child. I was no longer a member of the younger generation. Now, I was a member of the older parental generation tasked with providing wisdom and encouragement to a younger generation whose lives were rapidly changing even as I was quickly preparing to enter the latter half of my own life.

"How can I possibly be that?" I wondered aloud to my friend, feeling I was just drifting about like a sailboat on a placid sea without wind or rudder. It took me awhile to realize I was experiencing the disorientation of grief, which included the loss of the narrative I had been using to claim my identity, the meaning of my life and the way I lived in the world. The narrative I had been using to understand the world around me no longer held the same meaning or made sense to me because nearly everything had changed with the death of my parents. Now, I had to create a new narrative yielding a new identity with a new meaning and purpose for my life and a new way of living in the world based upon that new narrative and identity.

Soon after the coffee shop conversation I realized that the small membership congregations I have been serving, in fact many other congregations, are experiencing this same grief-based disorientation as they confront significant times of change and transition. They are like the traveler in the Robert Frost poem who comes to a fork in the road and wonders which road to take. Of course, Frost's traveler does make a choice. Unfortunately, some congregations in North America sense their journey has taken such an unexpected and disorienting turn that they are paralyzed: looking first down one road, then the other, without ever choosing a road to travel down. They are, very simply, lost in the forest of change and transition with very few guides to help them re-orient themselves onto the path leading to a thriving future of wholeness.

Congregations arrive at these forks in the road because of a whole matrix of changes impacting their community life. These changes range from the normal event of a pastor leaving the congregation due to retirement to a steep decline in membership. Or, because of demographic changes in their neighborhoods due to gentrification, a growing diversity of cultures, or the abandonment of the neighborhood by the people who created the neighborhood. These changes might also include being an aging congregation without any children present in worship or Sunday school. It may, also, be the growing poverty of a congregation, or an inability to discern how to re-purpose a building for new ministries and generating income. Of course, such change may also come from more traumatic experiences such as the misconduct of a pastor or lay leader, the death of a pastor or significant lay leader in the congregation, or a community-wide disaster that overwhelms the entire community. Any one of these changes, or any combination of them, are compounded by the overarching cultural changes impacting every aspect of North American culture like the movement from modernity to postmodernity or the movement from an analog-based culture to a digital-based culture.

The result of my personal experience of grief, coupled with my work of serving congregations experiencing the paralysis of disorientation, is the awareness that congregations caught up in this disorientation need a path guiding them through their grief. A path guiding congregations to answer the "why do we exist as a community of faith and who are we" identity questions while at the same time guiding them to discover the meaning or purpose for their communal lives, a purpose which congregations can intentionally live.

Also, it will be a path guiding congregations to discover that change and transition is a positive time for growth in the natural cycle of life. Of course, congregations will, also, discover living through change and transition does take time because the culture of the congregation is shifting to a new culture with either new traditions or older traditions being reframed to fit the new identity and congregational culture.

Unfortunately, after reading many of the great number of resources purporting to guide congregations through the interim period between installed pastorates or to guide them through transformation, revitalization, or redevelopment, I have discovered that none of them adequately address the process of change, the emotions of transition, particularly the deep and profound effect and influence of grief. Nor, do they speak about the importance of narrative for forming and shaping individual and community identity and the meaning and purpose for human life. Particularly, the resources fail to place importance on the biblical narrative as essential for forming and shaping Christian communities and the biblical narrative's ability to act as a catalyst for whole and thriving congregations.

What is needed is a different way of guiding congregations through the journey of change to reclaim the call to be communities who are healthy, thriving bodies of Christ engaged in *missio Dei*, God's mission to the world. This new way of guiding congregations will act as a catalyst for congregational transformation by taking seriously the process of change, the time of transition and the effect and influence grief has on congregations. It will reclaim the biblical language to help congregations articulate their emotions of grief and joy as well as help them re-orient themselves to their changed life situation.

Finally, it will tap into the power of narrative to weave the threads of their personal and congregational life stories and the biblical life story into a new holistic tapestry of life resplendent with the vibrancy, the joy, and the wonder of a transformed life.

Chapter 1

Change and Transition: Two Sides of the Same Coin

"We want to be transformed, but we don't know what that means," said Ernie, a member of the Pastor Nominating Committee (PNC) meeting with me to discern whether I was the person they would call to serve the congregation of First Presbyterian Church, Gloversville, New York.

At first glance First Presbyterian Church, Gloversville, looked like many old stately downtown churches. The red brick and the tall steeple looked elegant while the rest of the building took up most of the city block. The sign in the front of the church identified it not only as a Presbyterian congregation, but a congregation that had a staff and church office. Obviously, this was a church built to last and to be one of the anchors for the downtown city center. The members of this congregation had, over the years, been among the city's business and professional leaders.

It was only when one stepped close to the building that one saw that the bricks needed to be re-pointed because the mortar was crumbling or had fallen away. It was only when one was about to walk up the steps to the church that one saw the weeds standing as tall as the pretty flowers in the flowerbed. Then, at the top step one saw that the purple-blue doors were faded from the sunlight and no one had changed the message on the sign since World Communion Sunday three weeks before.

When one entered the building, it was easy to see that the walls needed a fresh coat of paint, that the flyers on the bulletin boards were advertising church and community events that had happened months before, and that the paint on the hallway walls was flaking badly and needed to be scraped and sanded. Then, as one walked down the stairs leading to the Fellowship Hall one was told, as I was by the PNC, that they had stopped using the Fellowship Hall and the second floor about five years ago because most of the parishioners were older and going up and down stairs was "just too difficult."

It would be very easy to look at the building, listen to the desire for transformation, calculate the average age of the parishioners at around 70-80, look at the worshipping community of 30-40, and weigh the possibilities for growth and success, then conclude, "No, I don't believe God is calling me to serve here."[1]

A little over 11 years ago, I arrived at a different answer. I heard in the desire for new life the small, still voice calling me to serve here. I knew this was my call because it was the place where my heart's passions and the world's needs converge. I knew the difficult challenge this congregation faced to "be transformed" based upon my own life experiences, my study, and my previous ministry. That challenge wasn't simply that they didn't know what being transformed meant nor was it only the dilapidated appearance of a building built more than 150 years ago. Rather, the challenge comprised the whole variety of issues this congregation was facing.

First, there was the decline in membership that mirrored the decline in the city's population and the decline in the economic base of the community. According to the U. S Census, the population of Gloversville was estimated at 15,243 in 2005, down 4,434 from 1970's census of 19,677. In addition, of the city's 6,500 households, 3,501 lived below the poverty line (U.S. Census 2005, Manning's Gloversville and Johnstown Directory 1971, 20). In the same period of time, the membership of the congregation declined from 505 active members to 142 active members (Session minutes 1978, 2004). Yet, the city's population and economic problems were not the only reasons for the congregation's membership decline. The death of congregational leaders and conflicts within the congregation occurred during this same time and these factors, also, contributed to the membership decline.

Second, all the churches in the community were marginalized. They were no longer the center of the city's cultural or civic life, nor were the pastors considered as part of the community's leadership. Indeed, the churches and the pastors were largely ignored except for the community Thanksgiving Day dinner, which was free to anyone who showed up to eat and during the Veterans' Day parade when a pastor was asked to sit in a car and wave to the crowd. In addition, the churches in the community were too overwhelmed by the complexity of the community's problems to actively pursue answers to the profound systemic issues emanating from and surrounding poverty, including drug and alcohol addiction, domestic violence, illiteracy, unemployment, and under employment.

This situation is congruent with Douglas John Hall's observation that one of the ways Christendom is changing its shape and form is its loss of power and influence as part of the "world's power elite" within Western societies. As Hall states very clearly, "This religion has been a great power in the world. It still can be regarded here and there as though its imperial status were yet intact, but it is nevertheless in the process of being reduced" (2).

Hall's contention is that Christendom is dying. It is not tied any longer to the imperial power structures of Western society, as it had been since the time of the Roman emperors, Constantine and Theodosius I. Thus, it has lost power and influence within many communities throughout North America and Europe (36).

The evidence of the Gloversville churches' loss of power and influence was visible when only the worship leaders attended the interfaith Thanksgiving Day worship service and the ecumenical Advent worship services. It was also evident when the Chamber of Commerce and the sole community newspaper failed to support a congregation's community-wide event exploring the possibility of the ways technology industries might add to the city's economic growth by opening up manufacturing plants or research centers that could employ city residents.

The lost power and influence of the Gloversville churches and Halls' analysis of the end of the imperial Christian church are part of the complex matrix of world-wide cultural change known as postmodernity.[2] No one can precisely pinpoint the beginning of this movement, but evidence of this seismic shift began showing up just after World War I and has accelerated since at least the 1950s. As Craig Detweiler and Barry Taylor remind us:

Postmodernity doesn't mean a mere adjustment of modernity. It is a quantum leap into a new world of ideas, values, and ethics. All of Western society has been impacted, and nothing is really the same. Rationalism, faith in the future, and many of the ideas that fueled modern Western life have been discarded, or at least, reinvented. (24)[3]

While few Americans have read the philosophical ideas of Jean Beaudrillard, Jacques Derrida, or the other postmodern thinkers, many are living the experience of the rapid changes and transitions just described (24). This is easily witnessed just by looking at the typical American family portrayed by television. Once it was "Leave It to Beaver" and "Ozzie and Harriet" in the 1950's, then it was Ozzy and Sharon

Osbourne in the "Osbournes" and Homer and Marge Simpson in the "Simpsons," in the 1990's and early 2000s and now it is "South Park" and the drama of the wealthy Kardashian family played out as so-called reality television. Yet, both "South Park" and the Kardashian family will also be supplanted as the typical American family because we live in an age when change and transition happen at the speed of light.

The rapidity of change and transition is also evident in the history of the industrial revolution that began in England then moved to the United States with boot factories and woolen mills outside of Boston, Massachusetts in the early 19th Century giving way to the mass production of automobiles and other consumer goods in the early 20th Century that has given way in the 21st Century to three dimensional printing of weapons and waffles in homes and offices. These industrial changes gave rise to new technology yielding space shuttles, high definition television, cell phones, and laptop computers. Medical advances in areas such as genetics carry much promise for human health and well-being, but also present ethical issues about designer babies and embryonic stem cell research. In addition, changes and transitions in employment and career patterns occur on a global scale as does connecting people around the world through Facebook, Twitter and blogs. All of these changes and transitions are creating a larger and denser understanding of community.[4]

Many Americans are also experiencing firsthand the intense questions postmoderns ask about relying upon the certainties of the Enlightenment that are based upon the ability of science, technology, and rational paradigms to solve every problem and make living better for humankind, if not for the rest of creation. Science and technology's failure to deliver on this promise, coupled with the erosion of the theoretical base upon which its mechanistic model for understanding the world was constructed, has created problems and discontinuities in every area of life. Currently, the conversation happening among theologians, pastors, academics, social and intellectual historians, anthropologists, educators, TED talk presenters and the media in their reporting of studies, articles, books and lectures seems aimed at a paradigm shift from a less mechanistic way of understanding the world in favor of a more holistic way or even a more organic notion about life. However, these current conversations are not monolithic, since there is great diversity among the conversation partners (Drane, 2000:8-9; Detweiler and Taylor:29-59; Coffey and Gibbs:17-39; Loughlin:3-26; Heelas and Woodhead:1-11).

When one examines this complex matrix of cultural, community and congregational change and transition, it is clear that the people of First Presbyterian were caught in the change and transition cycle that is a natural part of life. The cycle begins when a life situation or relationship ends and is only complete when a new beginning takes hold, becoming the new way of being for the person, the family, the organization or the congregation.

Unfortunately, change and transition are not well understood by most persons, families, organizations or congregations. This is evident in the high failure rate of planned change efforts in business organizations and congregations and how often change and transition are not included in topics for study in graduate business degree programs, graduate education programs and seminary degree programs, all of which are designed to create new leaders, who will lead efforts to change, revitalize or transform those very organizations and communities of faith.

This makes comprehending what is meant by change and the change process and transition and the transition process critical components for leading persons, families, organizations and congregations through this natural, recurring cycle to the new thriving and sustainable future they all desire.

Change happens all the time and all around us. The seasons change from spring to summer to fall to winter. We see changes in ourselves whenever we look at the family photographs posted on Facebook, Instagram, Snapchat or YouTube. When change happens transition also happens because change and transition are two sides of the same coin and cannot be separated discretely into little components because human beings cannot be discretely separated into little components and still be living, thriving beings. It is like thinking that when we heal a person's body it has nothing to do with the person's mind, emotions or spirituality. Of course, when we treat one portion of the person we are treating the whole person and this understanding has slowly made its way back into the practice of medicine and into the teaching of medicine in medical schools and nursing schools. Thus, leading change is really leading the change in a physical life situation and the emotional and spiritual response to that change in the physical life situation. To focus on one without focusing on the other at the same time is setting up individuals, families, organizations or congregations for the failure to thrive.

So, what do we mean when we say the words "change and transition?"

Change, as I describe it, is the shifting material life conditions of persons, families, organizations and communities that requires an adjusting response from a person, family, organization or community. Everyone will experience change, and their response to that change will dictate whether they are imprisoned in the present and the future by the past or they are set free to discover the path to a thriving and sustainable future.

Change may be planned like a wedding, a graduation, retirement, creating a new product line or starting a new genre of worship. Change may be unplanned like disease, accidents, hurricanes, pregnancy, birth, being laid off from work or being caught engaging in inappropriate behavior.

All of these are a shift in a material life condition and each one requires a response to that shift. Change theorists have proposed a number of models to respond to these shifts in material life conditions from Kurt Lewin's integrated Field Theory, Group Dynamics and 3 Step Model to Ronald Lippett's seven step model. In addition, a five step model has been developed, John Kotter created an eight step model, Practitioners of social cognitive behavior change have their model and Everett Roger developed a 5 Step Diffusion model of change. In nursing practice literature, Prochaska and Di Clemente have described a spiral model to be used in patient care while the Aspen Institute's Theory of Change model is available as a computer fill-in-the blanks product for community activists. More recently, a 6 Step Changeology model of change has been published in a book. (Kritsoni 1-7, Mitchell 32-37, Kotter 55-65)

What all of these models have in common is they are all about planned change. They are all rational, they are all goal centered, they focus on human behaviors, and they give leadership advice for those leading change. Also, they all admit the change process is not quick and is likely to fail if those leading change do not attend to every one of the components or steps.

Taking John Kotter's *Eight Step Process of Successful Change* as an example, those leading or proposing a planned change begin by:

1. Create a sense of urgency by helping others see the need for change and the importance of acting immediately.

2. Pull together the guiding team making sure there is a powerful group guiding the change with leadership skills, credibility, communications ability, authority, analytical skills and a sense of urgency.

3. Develop the change vision and strategy that will clarify how the future will be different from the past, and how you can make that future a reality.

4. Communicate for understanding and buy-in, so many people in the organization or community understand and accept the vision and strategy.

5. Empower others to act by removing barriers, so those who want to make the vision a reality can do so.

6. Produce short term wins by creating visible, unambiguous successes as soon as possible.

7. Don't let up on moving forward with the change by pressing harder and faster after the first successes. Be relentless with initiating change after change until the vision is a reality.

8. Make it stick by recognizing you are creating a new culture by holding on to the new ways of behaving and making sure they succeed until they become strong enough to replace old traditions.

As one reads the full discussion of each of these steps in Kotter's books or reads the writings of the other change theorists discussed above it becomes apparent that the planned change process is complex and that what change is really doing is creating a new culture in an organization or community with a new identity and a new purpose. What is also apparent is that the planned change process is not about tinkering around the edges by addressing a few behaviors. Planned change will be disruptive, will demand more learning of how to think differently, and may displace persons from one position of status to a different position of status either higher or lower within the organization, community, or an individual's perception of themselves.

Additionally, it is clear the planned change process is not a quick fix or a short term process, but will take a 7 to 10-year period to come to complete fruition, which is one reason why most planned change fails (Kotter 66, Buchanan et al: 191). Organizations, communities, families and individuals simply become too anxious to have the process completed as though planned change is like ordering a hamburger from McDonalds or Burger King (Kotter 66, Buchanan et al: 191-201). In addition, organizations and communities frequently get rid of the people leading the change or articulating the vision for change either through firing them, promoting them or retiring them, ensuring the change effort will stop. (Buchanan et al:194-201).

The other reason most planned change fails is none of the planned change processes fully consider the emotional response integral to all change, planned or unplanned, that is called transition, which is the other side of the coin of change.

Transition is the emotional and spiritual response that perceives a shift in the material condition of life as an ending that is experienced as a death. Like all deaths, endings are subject to the disorientation of grief and a time of fertile emptiness leading to reflection about who the person, the community of faith or the organization is now. Actively grieving for what has ended gives people the opportunity to acknowledge that the ending has happened, that it is painful and that feelings of confusion and being set adrift in the world without direction are real. The time of fertile emptiness is a time to ask questions such as why do I exist? Why am I doing what I am doing? Why is what I am doing important to me, to my family or to the community where I live? Deep reflection seeks to answer these questions and uncover a vast universe of possibilities for a thriving and sustainable future. This deep reflection is the beginning movement toward a re-orientation of comprehending how the world works now and the creation of a new identity and the meaning for life flowing from that new identity, according to William Bridges. Disorientation, fertile emptiness and re-orientation are the trail markers signaling the turning points on the path to a new, thriving life. Indeed, Bridges states, "they are the key times in the natural process of self-renewal" (5).

Chapter 2

The Forest of Change and Transition

All change and transition start with an ending. How that ending is handled is critical because it is the precondition for renewal. Endings begin when people are disengaged from the contexts in which they have known themselves. "This may occur through divorce, death, job changes, moves, illnesses, and many other lesser events," states Bridges (95). Disengagement breaks the old cue-system, which had served to reinforce the roles used to pattern the person's or the congregation's behavior. During disengagement the way a person or congregation defined themselves is lost creating the sensation of "not quite being sure of whom they are anymore" (96). The inability to define one's self is like losing the thread of one's life story which leads to the loss of one's identity which in turn leads to the loss of the meaningfulness for life. Here in this ending is the disorientation that comes with disengagement. The sensing that in some way reality is no longer the reality the person or persons thought it was, such as when we discovered the tooth fairy wasn't real "or that parents sometimes lie, act silly, are afraid, and make mistakes, and that best friends let you down" (99).

Disorientation makes one feel like they are floating free in a kind of limbo where one is trying to find, once again, the anchor making the world real. However, before we can find the anchor, we need to let go of the way we understand the world to be and go below the surface of reality to seek a deeper understanding of ourselves, our relationships, and the world around us. It is important to state here that the willingness to go below the surface of reality and become more self-aware is critical. As Bridges notes, those people who do not choose to look beyond their old perspectives and beliefs, become merely disillusioned and will simply seek out replacements for what has ended that fit the old broken down views of the world without transformation or renewal taking place (99).

Disillusioned people are like the man who walks down a street and falls into a hole. After a while he gets out. Then, he walks down the same street and falls into the same hole. He gets out more quickly. He continues to walk down the same road falling into the same hole time and time again without ever realizing that he might want to walk around the hole or walk down a different street (Nelson, 3).

What Bridges is describing in disorientation is in reality grief. Something in our lives has died whether it is a relationship, a career, or a congregation's vitality and place within the larger society. This death stirs within us a multitude of diverse emotions that erupt into actions such as uncontrollable weeping and angry shouting, often erupting without warning and without apparent reason. This experience of grief is painful, but it is an experience which must be not be denied or tamped down into some pseudo managed place within ourselves where we think positive thoughts and try holding despair at bay by "lighting matches and whistling in the dark" (Bridges 103). If it is not lived through fully and acknowledged for what it is, then it will render us unable to be healed, renewed or transformed.

Even though the truth of that last statement is well known through the work of trauma specialists and, especially, Elisabeth Kubler-Ross in her seminal work *On Death and Dying*, resistance to living through and fully experiencing the pain, the anger, frustration, confusion, and the tears of grief is commonplace. Indeed, Elisabeth Kubler-Ross notes in *On Death and Dying* that we live in a culture that denies death and in denying death also denies the accompanying pain of grief. It is not surprising then that denial is the first stage in her outline of the stages of grief.

In addition, Walter Brueggemann in his work with psalms of lament notes that this unwillingness to confront the reality of grief may be one reason why we fail to read the psalms of lament: we find we cannot manage and control the pain, the suffering, and uncertainties that are all part of grieving. (1984:83)

The denial of grief is manifest as a drive to not change, to continue to be the same person or congregation we've always been, and to continue doing all the old familiar things we have always done. The seven last words of the church - "we've always done it this way before"- and its companion phrase - "and we aren't going to do it that new way" - speaks loudly about congregations' unwillingness to live through their grief. Other phrases similar to the church's seven last words say the same thing – "we are not going to give up what is familiar even if it is leading us to being imprisoned in a past we cannot change and which will not lead us to a thriving and healthy present and future."

Endings are experiences of dying and they do challenge our understanding of who we are as well as the meaning and purpose for our life. But endings are not the finality of our lives. As Bridges quotes Mircea Eliade, a student of passage rituals in diverse cultures, "In no rite or myth do we find the initiatory death as something final, but always as the condition *sine qua non* of a transition to another mode of being, a trial indispensable to regeneration, that is, to the beginning of new life" (110).

Coupled with the grief-based disorientation is the awareness that one has entered unfamiliar territory that seems to be an empty place where one is separate from the world. This may be imagined as a forest or a wilderness, but it may, also, be actual time spent away from familiar things, relationships, and routines such as the long weekend in a different city, a cabin in the woods or time spent at a retreat center. However, it is imagined and experienced, this is a time for the rest, reflection and discernment necessary to be re-energized, for learning new things about ourselves as we begin seeking a deeper knowledge about ourselves and our lives by asking questions such as: "What is the meaning of the actions I am taking? What will I do tomorrow and what will be the outcome of my life? How am I living toward the fulfillment of my life?" (118).

Intentionally seeking answers to these questions and others like them are the first steps toward re-orienting our lives to the new beginning that is about to take place. This new beginning may occur in a variety of ways, but it happens when one starts doing those actions that lead to the new beginning (134-150).

Chapter 3
The Usual Guides through the Forest

The characteristic shape of the transition process of disorientation, fertile emptiness, and re-orientation happen in the middle of change, planned or unplanned, and it is clear that persons or congregations who are still wandering lost in the forest or standing paralyzed at the fork of the road are having difficulty traversing their particular forest of transition. They need a guide to help them deal effectively with their ending as well as provide the path toward their new beginning that is integrated within the change process.

There is a plethora of contemporary resources for personal, family, organizational, community and congregational revitalization, transformation or redevelopment[5] and all claim to be the one resource that will prove useful in making their journey through change and transition. However, a review of these resources just for congregations uncovers significant problems.

First, they narrow down the reasons congregations are in change and transition to one of three: (1) contemporary culture is in the midst of a change from modernity to postmodernity and the problems plaguing congregations can be attributed solely to that cultural change; (2) the need for change is located within the congregation because of unhealthy relationships between members, or unnamed fears, or low commitment, or other ill-defined issues; (3) the problem is ineffective pastoral leaders who lack vision or lack the ability to clearly articulate their vision(Bandy:15-29; Rarick:5-7; Barna:11-16; Avery:1-15; Grossman, Sellon, Smith: ix-xvii; Nicholson: ix-xviii).

Second, the solutions offered by nearly all of those addressing congregational transformation may seem varied and unique, but they all rely upon the same methodologies of modernity that focus on predictability, quantification, efficiency, and control, which have been identified as one of the contributing causes to the need for congregational transformation. This is something akin to only having a hammer for a tool, making every problem a nail to be pounded.

I think looking at a representative sample of these resources is helpful to highlight the discussion. Tom Bandy in his work *Moving Off the Map* decries the same old church structure and energy sapping, committee dominated strategic planning process used by most decaying congregations. He then proceeds to outline a process for renewal using a highly complex, lengthy committee-task force-focus group that utilizes demographics and statistical analysis to determine congregational identity and community identity (15-29, 43-62).

Robert Craig and Robert Worley, in *Dry Bones Live*, depend upon questionnaires and marketing strategies that are focused on data gathering and analysis (20-31). Judith Rarick in *Into the Future*, describes the mixed use of Precept's ReVision program, which uses questionnaires, small groups, and marketing strategies relying heavily on statistics to provide a path for devising a congregational mission statement (4).

Gail Grossman, Mary Sellon and Daniel Smith, in *Redeveloping the Congregation*, develop a process for congregational redevelopment that is based upon John Kotter's model of change that was devised from the anecdotal study of 100 businesses that have undergone some organizational redevelopment. They, too, rely on committees, questionnaires, and statistical analysis as the pathway to redevelopment (1-21).

Bill Avery, in *Revitalizing Congregations*, discusses congregational revitalization through a focus on the creative power of pastors to single-handedly bring healing to congregations (1-15). The unstated implication in Avery's presentation is that lay leaders and congregations simply follow after the visionary pastor, who will lead them into their new future with very little need for the laity to develop their own initiatives for mission and ministry.

Roger Nicholson's work *Temporary Shepherds* is used as a training resource for interim ministers and he follows much of what Avery suggests is the role of the interim minister (1-13). Nicholson does outline some of the issues facing congregations in change and transition, but he fails to address the larger, complex emotional and cultural issues that also effect and influence congregations, particularly downplaying the need to engage congregational grief. George Barna, in *Without a Vision, The People Perish*, does move away from the foregoing voices of congregational transformation by emphasizing the need for a God-centered vision. However, he still maintains that the pastor is one who has the vision. The pastor then tells everyone else what the vision will be and how it will be carried out (11-16).

It is not simply that these transformation resources are tied to the methodologies of modernity that is problematic, but how their methodologies are tied to modernity's conception of human beings and communities in mechanistic terms. William Bridges outlines the description of humanity in mechanistic terms this way, "Surrounded as we are by industrial products, we have tended to treat everything as if its essential nature were that of a product...any changes that occur after [the product has been produced] are 'malfunctions' and signs that the mechanism needs repair" (30).

This description of human beings in mechanistic terms has led the above mentioned methodologies to be used as instruments in "undermining the essential human quest for personal fulfillment and meaningful spirituality" (Drane, 2001:26-27).

This connection becomes clear in the discussion of what sociologist George Ritzer describes as McDonaldization which is characterized as life on the industrial assembly line where:

Human beings, equipped with a wide array of skills and abilities, are asked to perform a limited number of highly simplified tasks over and over.

Instead of expressing their human abilities...people are forced to deny their humanity and act in a robot like manner. People do not express their humanity ...but rather deny themselves (8).

John Drane describes McDonaldization and its relationship to the church as "The church and the iron cage" (2001, 39) because the four characteristics of McDonaldization's iron cage are found within the church. These same four characteristics - efficiency, calculability, predictability, and control - are also found in the methodologies of modernity named above. A full discussion of these four characteristics reveals how they limit the use of human ability and skills.

Efficiency is simply the way to find the best means to reach a particular end. Efficiency is not by itself a bad thing; however, in an over-rationalized society the search for the best way to do things is often declared to have already been found and then it is institutionalized, which closes down any opportunity for people to discover on their own the best way to accomplish a particular task. This drive for efficiency has created congregational transformation resources that are similar to each other, starting with describing the process of transformation and the reasons for transformation. They also share the same methods for engaging the transformation process, such as demographic studies, small committees to do strategic planning, advertising, and creating a mission statement that is given to the congregation. In addition, they are pre-packaged, quick-fix programs that claim to contain everything a congregation needs to be successful (Bandy 15-29, 43-62, Craig and Worley 20-31, Rarick 4-25, Grossman, Sellon, and Smith 1-21). These resources and programs are the theological and spiritual equivalent of fast food. It comes to you quickly without you doing any preparation and is convenient, but in the end it has no nutritional value and is incapable of sustaining life.

Calculability, on the other hand, is all about size and quantification. This is reflected in reliance on demographics, statistical analysis and measuring congregational vitality and health based on such statistics as the number of people sitting in the pews or the number of children in Sunday school and youth group. The focus on quantitative analysis also feeds the anxiety over membership decline and the age of those sitting in the pews that is expressed by statements like, "we have to get more young families here on Sunday morning."

This anxiety comes from congregations being taught there is a correlation between church health and vitality and the number of members in a congregation. This teaching comes from the culture, both inside and outside of Christianity, that highlights the megachurches like Willow Creek Community Church, Saddleback Church, and Peachtree Presbyterian Church. This teaching also comes from the constant refrain from mainline denominations about how they are shrinking in membership that is reported in newspaper articles, articles from Christianity Today and denominational publications and letters from denominational leaders. In addition, there is the constant cultural conditioning of a consumer-oriented society to equate success and wellbeing with large numbers, i.e. best movie makes the most money, the best actor is the one who makes the most money, the bestselling book is a must read, and the bestselling exercise video must get you thinner and leaner faster. All of this leads the folks in congregations to conclude that healthy and vital churches that are "really doing ministry" are those with large numeric growth that any congregation can attain if they just do what these other growing churches are doing.

This leads to the third characteristic of McDonaldization, which is predictability; the ability to know what to expect in all settings and in all times. This desire for predictability has led to the proliferation of chain restaurants, hotels, and other similar retail establishments because consumers could be assured that, wherever they traveled in the United States, they would find the comfort of a familiar, seemingly reliable eating or shopping experience. Predictability can create a sense of security and safety, but it can also lead to routine and can be used to stop a healthy exchange of views by imposing homogeneity upon congregations, so that members are not challenged to think deeply. It can be used by those in power to maintain control.

Control is the final characteristic of McDonaldization and goes hand in hand in with the other characteristics, since those characteristics can only be maintained by a small cadre of leaders wielding the power to control what happens. Unfortunately, for many congregations the one who has held the power is the pastor, who determines the vision and the ministry that will be accomplished, while lay ministry becomes nothing more than the equivalent of pumping your own gas or packing your own grocery bags. This same phenomenon occurs when a single powerful lay leader or group of lay leaders exercises power and control to keep the congregation from changing, despite a pastor who may have a vision and plan for change (Drane, 2001, 53).

As important as the critiques of the methodologies of modernity and McDonaldization, and the lack of understanding about the importance of the transition process are, what is equally important is the failure of contemporary transformational resources to even consider the power of narrative to form and shape individuals and communities. This failure is particularly evident in the congregational transformation resources previously discussed.

Chapter 4

Reclaiming Story-telling for Change and Transition

Humans have been telling stories since the first prehistoric cave drawings of hunts all the way to the movies released last week. As novelist Douglas Coupland writes, "It's not healthy to live life as a succession of isolated little cool moments. Either our lives become stories, or there's just no way to get through them...this is why the three of us left our lives behind us and came to the desert--to tell stories and to make our lives worthwhile tales in the process" (1991:8, 23-24). Coupland makes the case in his novel *Generation X: Tales for an Accelerated Culture* for the power of narrative to speak about our lives in the context of family, culture, tradition, and language. Narrative can unfold both personal identity and communal identity by bringing together the diverse experiences of life into a coherent whole that is the key to discovering meaning for life.

Indeed, Alasdair McIntyre asserts that the concept of selfhood is the concept of a unified self residing "in the unity of a narrative which links birth to life to death as a narrative beginning to middle to end" (1981:90). When we are attempting to understand what is happening in our lives or the lives of others we often begin by telling a story. McIntyre suggests this begins with even the very simple act of observing a man digging in a garden. We ask, "What is he doing?" which then can lead to any number of answers that may or may not be true, but they all need a narrative to answer the question (90).

McIntyre further reminds us that human life is lived within a narrative, a narrative we enter from our birth, since the world existed before we were born. We are not the creators of our own lives; rather we are those who are created and we find our place within this larger narrative through our parents teaching us the communal narrative, including its history, traditions, and its values. This communal narrative shapes our life experience by giving us an identity and meaning for life, which we live as part of an interlocking set of stories (101-104; Drane, 2001:155; Bradt:3-19).

Thus, stories are the way humans define themselves, orient themselves to living within the world and understanding their relationship with the world. Narratives become what Stephen Crites describes as "dwelling places where people are living their lives" (70). This echoes the well-known Nguni Bantu proverb, "I am because we are, we are because I am," since it too speaks about how we know ourselves through being part of a community as well as how we influence the communal narrative by our participation in it. It also echoes the Irish proverb, "It is in the shelter of each other that people live," which speaks to the connection of one person to the other persons in the community tied together by the stories the community shares. As Archbishop Tutu has said in his 2004 work "Ubuntu", "The essence of being human [is] that you can't exist as a human being in isolation. It speaks about our interconnectedness. You can't be human all by yourself. We think of ourselves far too frequently as just individuals, separated from one another, whereas you are connected and what you do affects the whole world."

Our participation in the community and our sheltering within the community comes as we find that one aspect of stories' power is they are multi-layered and have the ability to be open-ended and flexible. When a story is told, then re-told, each teller has the ability to add or shift meaning through gestures and vocal emphasis. This makes it possible for the story to grasp the listener or reader and bring them into a story that speaks concretely about their life experience, whether of pain, disconfirmation, or affirmation. Thus, one might see each person as a story in progress, seeing the person's uniqueness and the wholeness of their life story in the context of the present moment as they describe their life experience (124-125 Burkhardt and Nagai-Jacobson). This also opens up the possibility for two people to tell their individual stories to each other, discovering the places where their stories overlap with each other. Then, in that moment, they experience their stories weaving together until there becomes one new story connecting these two people together by the threads of a new tapestry (Bradt:39-49).

For example, consider the opening verses of Jeremiah 1:1-5

The words of Jeremiah son of Hilkiah, of the priests who were in Anathoth in the land of Benjamin, to whom the word of the Lord came in the days of the King Josiah son of Amon of Judah in the 13th year of his reign. It came also in the days of King Jehoiakim son of Josiah of Judah, and until the end of the 11th year of King Zedekiah son of Josiah of Judah, until captivity of Jerusalem in the fifth month. Now the word of the Lord came to me saying, "Before I formed you in the womb I knew you, and before you were born I consecrated you; I appointed you a prophet to the nations.

Here in this brief passage we learn a great deal about Jeremiah. We know the essential relationships of his life. First is God's relationship with Jeremiah in his mother's womb and second is his relationship with his family in Anathoth, who are priests. Indeed, we find out his father's name and his tribe. We also learn that he was writing before and until Jerusalem was captured and the people sent into exile, so we have a historical time when he lived. Here we have the beginnings of a relationship with this prophet who lived about 2,700 years ago. When we read further, we learn more about him and the depth and characteristics of the relationship he has with God and his community. We learn how his relationship with God influences and impacts his relationship with the community and how his relationship with the community influences and impacts his relationship with God as the prophet lives his identity and the purpose for his life stated in the very small scripture passage quoted above. We also discover through reading his story the way his life and our lives overlap in the experiences we share.

For example, when I closely read and studied Jeremiah in seminary I was surprised to find a connection between the way God called the prophet and how God called me into ministry as well as how God's call shaped my life and the relationships of my life in similar ways to the prophet. I have often felt many of the prophet's own emotions such as feeling that I'd rather not have a particular call to serve a particular congregation or that sometimes I felt ignored by the people God sent me to serve. This resonance of my life with the prophet's life has created a connection between Jeremiah and me that has drawn me into the biblical narrative and made it part of my life story as much as my life story has become part of the biblical story of life because I, too, am part of God's people, past, present and future.

As a retired teacher from a congregation I served said, "Stories interact with other stories in our lives" to build narratives that include everyone in our lives. These larger narratives help us to create our lives through the lessons we learn from other people. "My dance teacher, "the retired teacher said, "taught me that people need to express themselves and I carried this over into my teaching in the way I taught my students." This is the reason she told her story about her dance teacher. It was the story about her dance teacher that helped me to understand the retired teacher's passion for encouraging people to find a way to express themselves, and remembering her story reminds me to do the same when I am teaching.

This is why community ancestral stories are not abstract or ideas to be proved true or false. They are a community's lived experience that becomes a community's life story expressed in music, dance, ritual or storytelling. The people in the community ritually enact these ancestral community stories, so they might embody the ancestral community story in the present as the overarching story or a meta-narrative of a community's identity and reason for existence (Jodock:134-135). These overarching stories, or meta-narratives, form the foundation for connecting the daily stories of each person's life within the community's life. When each person's life story is woven together with the community's life story a reality is created. In this reality, past, present and future come together to form an orientation to the world we tend to define as a world view (Crites:71; Drane 2001:155-156; Bradt:88-117).

However, there is not just one meta-narrative available for people to choose to join. There are multiple communities we have access and can learn from and each has its own narrative, whether of faith, politics, nation, state, family, ethnicity, or economics. What our meta-narrative is depends upon the community we choose to join (McIntyre, 1981:106-110).

This is congruent with my own study of Paul's letter to the Thessalonians when he reminds them that they have become a different people who have a new meta-narrative as the people of God. (See Appendix 2).

Despite some postmoderns' assertion that no one is seeking a meta-narrative, John Drane points out that "story is central to the contemporary quest for meaning, in much the same way as abstract analysis was central to the outlook of modernity" (2001:155-168). It is vitally important to realize that people are searching for a meta-narrative. A meta-narrative that will encompass their lives in such a way that they will have the ability to navigate through the turbulent waters of the present age when life seems to be fragmented, disjointed, and meaningless to find the place where they discover, once again who they are and why they are alive (2001:157). The acuteness of this search for a meta-narrative is stated clearly by Joan Didion in her essay quoted by Darrell Jodock,

It was not until we had passed Diamond Head and were coming in low over the reef for landing at Honolulu, however, that I realized what I most disliked about this incident: I disliked it because it had the aspect of a short story, one of those 'little epiphany' stories in which the main character glimpses a crisis in a stranger's life ...and is moved to see his or her own life in a new light. I was not going to Honolulu because I wanted to see life reduced to a short story. I was going to Honolulu because I wanted to see life expanded to a novel, and I still do. (130)

Jodock makes the point that people who are caught up in the disorientation of their lives are looking for "a coherent story to make sense of their lives, collectively and often individually as well" (130). A young woman named Lisa Baker put it this way,

"*All I want is reality. Show me God. Help me to understand why life is the way it is, and how I can experience it more fully and with greater joy.*

I don't want the empty promises. I want the real thing. And, I'll go wherever I find that truth system." (Drane, 2001:118)

McIntyre makes this same point when he speaks about what happens when the world changes and we discover that it is no longer exactly as we thought it to be. For example, when a person "who has believed that he was highly valued by his employers and colleagues is suddenly fired, or someone proposed for membership in a club whose members were all, so he believed, close friends is black balled" (1977:138). The question that is asked, according to McIntyre, is this: what happens when our knowledge of reality comes in conflict with the true reality of the world or comes into conflict with other ways of interpreting and understanding the world?

Here is the intersection where narrative and the transition process Bridges outlines meet. It is at this intersection where the power of narrative moves us through disorientation and the fallow time of transition to re-orient our lives in the present and the future by giving us the ability to discover a new way of knowing and understanding ourselves and the world. It is at this intersection where we discover new possibilities for living in the world (McIntyre, 1977:138-157; Bradt: 39-59).

Indeed, narratives have always been the means humans have used to define themselves and their communities, so their lives have meaning, purpose and coherence. Also, narratives have always been the way to guide individuals, families, and communities toward healing and reorienting their lives toward a new and thriving future by using the flexibility, open-ended and multi-layering aspect of stories to draw together the fragments, the disjointed experiences of life into a coherent whole. Humans have often thought life was coherent, reliable and filled with unchanging rules about the way life is "supposed to be" until that life becomes incoherent, unreliable, fragmented and broken apart like a wine glass that falls on a hardwood floor. This fragmentation and brokenness of life happens through trauma, through experiences of war that create moral injury, or even through the more mundane changes of aging, of people moving to new communities, of pastors retiring or seeking new pastoral positions in a new place. The work of creating a new story out of the broken fragments of the old story, of our past and present, is precisely what is experienced when reading the psalms of lament or the book of Lamentation.

Lament is the oral and written narrative about how life has become broken and fragmented, filled with pain and with the anguish of suffering spoken in words that are raw, angry, ragged, raging, impolite and dangerous. It asserts that the reliability of life may not be as reliable as the person speaking these words thought it was before this changed physical life experience and the disorientation of transition. Thus, the narrative the community has used may not be trusted to speak the whole truth of life. The psalms of lament and the book of Lamentation give us clear examples of, what Walter Brueggemann describes as, "the counter narrative to Israel's story of a well-ordered world that is reliable and governed by a loving God, who provides the necessities of life and protects Israel." The psalms of lament are filled with the rawness, the harsh and hard to utter words describing the pain of disorientation as the people speak aloud their grief in the midst of a community experiencing the unreliability of their life, where they speak the truth: a person or community's life is not able to be managed and controlled. (52-52, Brueggemann 1984)

One such psalm of lament is Psalm137:

By the rivers of Babylon—
 there we sat down and there we wept
 when we remembered Zion.
2 On the willows[a] there
 we hung up our harps.
3 For there our captors
 asked us for songs,
and our tormentors asked for mirth, saying,
 "Sing us one of the songs of Zion!"

*4 How could we sing the LORD's song
   in a foreign land?
5 If I forget you, O Jerusalem,
   let my right hand wither!
6 Let my tongue cling to the roof of my mouth,
   if I do not remember you,
if I do not set Jerusalem
   above my highest joy.*

*7 Remember, O LORD, against the Edomites
   the day of Jerusalem's fall,
how they said, "Tear it down! Tear it down!
   Down to its foundations!"
8 O daughter Babylon, you devastator!* [h]
   *Happy shall they be who pay you back
   what you have done to us!
9 Happy shall they be who take your little ones
   and dash them against the rock! (NRSV)*

This psalm tells the story of a change in the psalmist's physical life experience by the trauma of war and of exile, which is echoed in the book of Lamentation, with language that reveals the transition emotions of disorientation and the anger of grief in the wilderness, actual and figurative, of change and transition. While the psalms of lament speak the truth about grief and disorientation, nearly all of the psalms of lament contain a turn toward celebration and affirmation of a new beginning where life is once again filled with the joy and hope of a renewed future. This turn is the place where God has intervened to end the disorientation and bring the psalmist to the dawn of a renewed future marked by praise and gratitude to God for awakening this psalmist to new possibilities for life.

None of the psalms detail exactly what God has done to move the psalmist out of the depths of disorientation, perhaps because what was done is not as important as the reality that God did intervene on behalf of a renewed life. Perhaps, what is most important is in the midst of the wilderness of transition a new beginning and a new future was made available for the psalmist like a door swinging open with the invitation for the person to cross over the threshold and begin living their new future.

This is the intersection of narrative and the change and transition process where we discover narrative to be the underlying foundation for guiding congregations through their times of change and transition. However, not just any narrative will do for congregations because Christians are formed and shaped by the particularity of the biblical narratives.

"A congregation is Christian to the degree that it is confronted by and attempts to form its life in response to the Word of God," insists William Willimon (11).

Willimon's insistence on scripture echoes Richard H. Niebuhr's contention that "Christianity is based upon the life story of the community of disciples both as individuals and as a community and not on the dogmas and abstract metaphysical systems, ideals or imperatives. These abstractions have been poor substitutes for the New Testament and when the church has fed on abstractions it has become "subject to spiritual rickets. (Niebuhr 23)." Niebuhr continues to speak about the importance of story by comparing the way objective history is not a substitute for personal life stories that draw people into an understanding of what has happened. He compares Lincoln's Gettysburg address with a standard historian's writing about the same event. He also makes the point that life stories happen within contexts where the meaning of these stories give shape to the meaning of life for persons and communities. He also makes it clear that God is the God who transcends history, but who is also involved in history and that God is revealed within the lives of people, such as Abraham, Isaac, and Jacob as well as other persons. God is not subject to only the Scriptures, but is revealed in the lives of other persons beyond scripture. Thus, God's history reaches beyond what is written in scripture, entering into the lives of people throughout the world where the experience of God is based upon their testimony in the story of their lives (Niebuhr 30).

Both Willimon and Niebuhr affirm that the Bible is a reality-defining narrative that stands against other competing narratives for understanding not only how the world was put together, but also how it works and how people are to live together in community. This reality is defined each Sunday when the people journey from their homes and gather together in a sanctuary to hear once more the biblical narrative read and proclaimed through the whole of liturgy. This reality lives in the waters of baptism and the celebration of Eucharist where we are called to remember God's mighty acts of salvation by reliving God's saving act of grace in Jesus Christ's death on a cross and his resurrection to new life.

"We are a storied people," says Stanley Hauerwas, because "the God that sustains us is a 'storied God" (35, 89-92).[6]

The change and transition process I have developed for congregations takes seriously the change and transition process and the power of narrative. It, also, takes seriously Willimon's insistence on the Word of God, Niebuhr's challenge to let go of dogma and abstraction in favor of narrative, and Hauerwas' claim that we are a storied people of a storied God. Further, this process affirms the promises narrative theology holds out for the revelatory power of the biblical narrative to create a new path for congregations caught in change and transition to walk into their new thriving, healthy, and sustainable future.

This new path weaves together the biblical narrative and the congregational narrative into one holistic story that will act as a catalyst for a transformative experience that builds community. It encourages a congregation to create a community that is willing to be vulnerable with others, a community respecting and cherishing the vulnerability of others, and a community that is a place of healing, health, vitality, compassion, hope, and learning. This new community will intentionally reclaim the call to be a community of Christ engaged in missio Dei, God's mission to the world (Drane, 2001:156-173; Coffey and Gibbs:88-89).

Chapter 5

Weaving Narratives for New Life

The change and transition pathway I have designed is best described as immersing the congregation in an environment dominated by the interaction of the biblical narrative with their own personal and congregational narrative. The members of the community share their identity through storytelling by speaking about their community's past, present, and hope for the future using open ended questions that encourage people to tell stories of the community's past and present. This leads to a community developed statement of their identity and a renewed understanding of what they are called to do in ministry and mission because of who they are.

It is similar to learning to speak French by living in a small French village surrounded by those who already speak the language and whose culture is dominated by the French language. The result of immersing the congregation in such an environment is the weaving together of their narrative with the biblical narrative, which opens up a new way of knowing who they are, knowing the meaning and purpose God has for their lives, and empowering them to deepen their relationship with God by intentionally living their new identity and purpose.

I, also, take seriously the use of John Kotter's eight step process for change that recognizes:

* The need for urgency to engage the change and transition process.

*The shared leadership of members representing the diversity of the congregation.

*The creation of identity as the shared vision.

*Being transparent and communicating clearly using all the media available to the congregation whether print, electronic or verbal.

*Empowering the entire congregation to participate in creating the new congregational narratives and identity as well as evaluating whether current practices and processes are coherent with the new identity or need reframing or discarding.

*Celebrating when experiments with new missions, events or practices work well, while dispensing with the language of success or failure when they do not.

*Recognizing the change and transition process is a "lived into' journey from the ending through the fallow time of reflection and re-imagination until the congregation experiences the new beginning growing from infancy to maturity over the next seven to ten years. During this journey the congregation evaluates their rituals, favorite events, and practices. Some of which may be reframed and others may be discarded as no longer relevant for the congregation's thriving and sustainable future.

Six distinct elements comprise this change and transition process and all of them occur concurrently to provide a holistic approach to congregational life. These six elements are: worship, a six-week workshop series, educational activities, new missions, fellowship, and communication.

We begin with worship because it is central to the life of the gathered community. In worship, the gathered community acknowledges it comes together because Christ has claimed them and called them through the waters of their baptism and by the cross and resurrection to be a people united to Christ and to each other as Christ's body in the world. We affirm in worship that we are responding to God's grace experienced in Jesus Christ as the gift of new life. The gathered community further affirms their lives are centered in God yielding a distinctive way of living as scripture is read and proclaimed, the sacraments are celebrated, and prayers are spoken and sung. The weaving together of the biblical narrative of life and the community's life story happens during worship and is internalized, becoming a shared memory, vision and experience that sustains and nurtures the alternative consciousness of being the people of God in the world as well as sustaining and nurturing their witness of that consciousness to the world (Westeroff:41-68; Lathrop 1993:15-53; Saliers:276-283; Zimmerman:302-310).[7]

Sunday morning worship is structured as a narrative articulating the themes of orienting our lives to God, moving from lamentation to hope, God's promises of life and the renewed life in Jesus Christ's death and resurrection, and God doing a new thing. This narrative begins with the people gathering to offer praise and thanksgiving to God, then moves to scripture, sermon and Eucharist at the middle of the narrative, then ends with the people going out into the world led by the light of Christ to live as the body of Christ in and for the world.

The importance of this narrative structure for worship became clear during a preaching series on the psalms using Walter Brueggemann's schema of orientation, disorientation, and re-orientation for three reasons. First, using the psalms of orientation the congregation begins to recognize the biblical narrative's claim that God has created a well-ordered, reliable world where life is created and sustained in a protected space God continues to preside over through generosity, faithfulness and steadfast love.

Second, the congregation experiences grief when life is broken, is no longer experienced as reliable and well ordered, is seemingly filled with suffering and raggedness, and the anchor for life has given way setting people drifting in disorientation. This disorientation is articulated in the raw, impolite, and truthful speech of the psalms of disorientation, better known as laments, that are an act of faith in God, who makes a way out of no way. Through the language of the psalms of disorientation the congregation hears and learns the language of lament as faithful and appropriate speech to articulate the pain of grief and suffering. Finally, the congregation hears in the psalms of disorientation that grief and disorientation are not the final answer because of the turn in the majority of these psalms affirming that God has heard the people's cries and has acted to change their situation. This affirmation is confirmed by the psalms of re-orientation celebrating the new life God has brought into being (15-28, 51-58, 123-125).

In addition, this narrative structure for worship complements and reinforces the learning goals for the six-week workshop series. Each workshop begins and ends with worship that is designed to be multi-sensory, emergent, participatory, contemplative, and challenging through the use of music ranging from Gregorian chant to Taizé, silence, and prayers from a variety of cultures and historical periods. The worship both leads into the theme of each workshop and it draws the participants toward the closure of each theme.

The workshops themselves are constructed around specific learning goals with each element of the workshop moving the participants toward the learning goals. The workshops use informal conversations around a circle, Bible study in small groups, teaching through playing games, sharing stories from their lives and sharing why the stories told are meaningful to them. In addition, participants walk through the community looking at the neighborhoods around the church to discern the possible needs of the community. Participants speak to leaders in the community to hear their perspective about community needs and issues. Also, participants review census data for their specific community to unlock the hidden issues and needs of the community. All of these actions lead the congregants to discuss what was seen, heard and gleaned followed by brainstorming possible solutions to the perceived community needs. Again, these responses to what was seen, heard and gleaned are told in story, though often people do not realize they are telling a story.

Coupled with worship and the workshops are educational activities that include a Bible study of the Psalms using Walter Brueggemann's schema of orientation-disorientation-re-orientation as a guide for the study. Ongoing Bible studies draw upon the biblical narrative to connect it with each participant's life by asking the question, "Where does this story show up in your life?"

Children and youth educational activities are linked to worship to create an opportunity for dialogue between teachers and students about what they heard and experienced in worship and the lesson being taught in either Sunday school or the youth group meeting.

The congregation's participation in missio Dei, God's mission to the world, is bound to worship and the workshops by the development of new ministries congruent with the congregation's new identity. This new identity, the "why" or reason for their existence, was formed during the workshop series and is connected to their passion for a particular ministry that is their response to hearing the call of Jesus Christ to be Christ's body actively engaged in ministries of justice, healing, peace, and reconciliation. Essentially, the congregation intentionally lives out its identity by doing those ministries that flow out from its identity and those ministries that witness to the Gospel in the places where the people of the community are located. Additionally, the congregation begins to evaluate everything they are doing through the lens of their identity with the result that those activities and ministries that are not coherent with their new identity are either reformulated or are discontinued, so that everything the congregation does and says is integrated into a whole.

The fifth element of the change and transition are the fellowship events formulated to reinforce the workshops, worship, educational activities and missio Dei. This also creates an environment for re-orienting the congregation's sense of time to the narrative rhythm of the Christian year from Advent to Christ the King Sunday through celebrations marking the passage of each season.

Finally, a variety of communication tools are used to report back to the congregation about what had happened during the workshops and to keep in front of the congregation their new identity. These communication tools are used to invite the congregation to participate in the new ministries.

Chapter 6

The Practical Example

The movement from the theoretical and conceptual to putting into practice the weaving of narratives for a thriving, healthy and sustainable community of faith is where the usefulness of the approach for congregational transformation becomes clear.

The practice begins with reclaiming the centrality of worship for forming and shaping the congregation through liturgy structured as a story with a beginning, middle and end, complementing the biblical narrative being told through scriptures, sermon, sung and spoken prayers, and the sacraments. This two-fold narrative order of worship is designed to weave together the biblical narrative and the congregation's narrative by asserting that God has gathered the people together and that God is the one whom the congregation is praising and thanking for the new life given to the congregation through the cross and resurrection of Jesus Christ. God is the one sending the congregation out to be the Body of Christ in the world. Thus, worship is God-centered and centered on the relationship between God and the people.

Also, the congregation by worshiping within this dual narrative order begins to experience what Gibbs and Coffey remind us happens every time the community of faith gathers together to worship God, keeping God at the center of worship; instead of devolving into entertainment or turning to the preoccupation of the human world of success and consumption, it places itself within the biblical narrative and joins their ancestors in worshipping God with praise and thanksgiving as their response to the truth of God's graciousness, holiness, and to acknowledge their dependence upon God (143-165).

In order to create the dual narrative order for worship, the order of worship is intentionally structured as a story. First, the welcome and announcements are placed at the beginning when the congregation gathers together. An intentional transition into worship is created by following the welcome with a contemplative prayer explicitly described as an invitation to the worshipping congregation to prepare to offer God praise and thanksgiving by centering their hearts and minds on God. This prayer explicitly begins telling the story and theme for the particular Sabbath worship. This prayer is followed by the prelude, then the call to worship, both of which continue telling the story and carrying the theme for the particular Sabbath worship.

Second, the prayers of the people are prayed among the people in the pews with the people invited and encouraged to pray aloud their concerns and intercessions as well as giving thanks aloud for the joys and blessings they had experienced. By this, the prayers become those arising from the midst of the people present in worship within the context of a prayer responding to the telling and the proclaiming of the biblical story of how God acted in the lives of people who are our ancestors in faith. This is the juxtaposition of old words to speak a new word of hope that Gordon Lathrop contends leads the congregation to a new way of understanding the world and a new way of conceiving and living their lives (1993:32).

Third, the word Eucharist is reclaimed to highlight the celebration of bread and wine arising out of our thanksgiving for God's grace given to all humanity through the cross and resurrection of Jesus Christ. Additionally, the Eucharist is placed after the reciting of the Apostles' Creed, which follows the reading of the biblical narrative and the sermon. This couples the Apostles' Creed and Eucharist as responses to the biblical narrative. Also, when Eucharist is celebrated, the prayers of the people occur in the middle of the Eucharistic prayer with the same invitation for the people present to pray aloud their concerns and intercessions. This creates another juxtaposition as the people relive God's creative acts of salvation in human history through the Eucharistic prayer of thanksgiving and offer prayers beseeching God's intervention in the lives of others in the present. We therefore express the trust that God is the one who hears people's cries for help in the past and in the present and witness to our trust that God not only hears the cries of people, but that God will act to transform the lives of people in the present just like God transformed the lives of people in the past. Here, is the place where the biblical narrative is woven into the congregational narrative bringing together past, present and future into a holistic moment that deepens the meaning of the sacrament and affirms the identity of those present as being God-centered people following Jesus Christ.

Fourth, the theme of hope is expressed throughout the liturgy from the call to worship and prayer of confession to the assurance of pardon and the prayer dedicating the offering to God for God's purposes in the world. The primary location for the exposition of the theme of hope is in the biblical narratives told and proclaimed in the sermon, which seeks to weave the biblical narrative and the congregation's narrative together in the preaching moment.

Finally, lay leadership in worship is made visible by the liturgists who lead portions of worship and acolytes who light the Christ candle. While the liturgists add adult, youth, and women's voices to worship, the children participating as acolytes add depth to worship by symbolically carrying the light of Christ into worship at the beginning, then carrying the light of Christ from worship out into the world with the congregation following Christ into the world at the conclusion of worship.

When a congregation I served talked about these changes in worship and why we were making them, one member of the congregation said she was glad, "we were focusing on God." And another said he was grateful for the "silent time to gather myself, so I could worship."

Still others recognized that "worship is part of who we are" and others said worship helped them recognize God's presence in the world around them. One woman in her seventies confirmed this by saying, "God permeates all matter, all life, everything." Another woman said, "Worship guides our lives," stating clearly her agreement with a quote from Rabbi Abraham Heschel, "Worship and living are not two separate realms. Unless living is a form of worship, our worship has no life" (Battin and Bell:131).

These last statements by the congregation confirm the need to be intentional about planning the order of worship for Sunday mornings. Underscoring the intentionality of planning worship suggests questions worship planners might ask: "Why do we worship this way?" "Why are we changing this or adding that?" And, most importantly, "Where is God in this?" Behind these questions is the desire to be authentic in worship as well as intentional.

The intentionality of worship planning and practice carries over into the intentionality of the second component of the process, the six-week workshop series.

The First Workshop

The first workshop session begins by asking nine open-ended questions designed to begin creating a congregational narrative. The first three questions will intentionally engage the congregation members in a conversation about the positive and negative aspects of their relationship with the former pastors. How these first questions are answered will provide clues to the congregation's grief and their willingness to actively grieve. Additionally, it will be a resource for the interim or currently installed pastor's pastoral care for the congregation by encouraging the congregation to grieve and tell the truth about relationships and their past. Also, the answers to these questions may open the door for deeper conversations about grieving, healing and ways to use the psalms of lament to contribute to the healing of grief. These questions will also help the congregation to begin telling their congregational life story by remembering and talking about their past, giving the interim or currently installed pastor clues to issues that have shaped and influenced this congregation's life over time. Indeed, the questions may shine a light upon the written congregational history, governing board minutes and newsletters that may become helpful in clarifying the congregation's relationship patterns, adding to the work the congregation needs to do in preparing for a new future.

The next four questions encourage the congregation to begin envisioning their future: who they want to be, how leadership of the pastor and lay leaders will influence and impact their future, the type of leadership needed and how they will intentionally begin writing this new chapter in the congregation's life story. These questions do not demand specific answers or actions at the present moment.

The final questions are designed to encourage the congregation to begin thinking about their place within the local and global communities and their impact upon the local and global communities, so they might begin to discover that they have a wider context for mission than they may have recognized previously. One might think of this part of the first workshop as day dreaming a new narrative into being.

Indeed, this whole first workshop session of the change and transition process is more about creating a congregational narrative than it is about the particular answers being given. As a matter of fact, this may be the first time congregational members have participated in a creative narrative process without the expectation of achieving a settled outcome. Thus, the critical aspect of this first workshop session for the facilitator, the interim pastor or the installed pastor is to use this time to actively listen to the conversation without trying to steer the conversation in any particular direction and without attempting to define or categorize the congregation's life story. Rather, the goal for the facilitator, interim pastor or installed pastor is to let the story unfold in the telling.

The Questions

1. What has the church's ministry of the last (x) years meant to you?

2. How have your expectations for the growth of the church's ministry been met?

3. How did all of the pastors' leadership influence the church's ministry? Or, not influence it?

4. What unmet expectations of the last (and current) pastoral relationship are still present?

5. What changes to the church's ministry either within the congregation or in the missions of the congregation would you make?

6. How will pastoral leadership and congregational leadership contribute to those changes?

7. What style of leadership is needed at this point in the congregation's life?

8. What will the local community lose if this community of faith ceases to exist?

9. How does this community of faith contribute to the global Christian church?

The Logistics for the First Workshop

The logistics for this first workshop session are fairly straightforward and easily accomplished. The congregation should be arranged into small groups of 10-15 participants each. If the congregation already has small groups, then these groupings can be used for this first workshop session. How these small groups are created is not particularly important. However, two members of the congregation's governing board should be appointed to aid in organizing the small group meetings. These meetings should be held in homes with light refreshments, so an informal environment is created that will stimulate conversation. Each small group should meet on successive evenings. For example, if there are 12 small groups then the meetings might begin with the first group meeting on Monday night, the next on Tuesday and the next on Wednesday and so forth until all groups have met. This schedule will place a demand upon the person facilitating the workshop, since that person will need to be at each small group meeting. However, it is a short term demand and cannot be effectively delegated.

The workshop facilitator will ask two participants to take notes during the meeting. These notes should, as much as possible, capture everything that is said at the meeting without editing. This is the reason for having two different people take notes, since each person may only capture a portion of the conversation. In addition, the workshop facilitator should have a newsprint pad of paper and easel and markers with the questions clearly written on the paper, so everyone can see the questions being asked. The workshop facilitator may take a few notes on the newsprint paper, but these should be limited to recurring themes or issues. The workshop facilitator is present to ask the questions, facilitate the conversation and, most importantly, to listen to what is being said.

The Outline of the Meeting (1-1.5 hours maximum)

1. Welcome, introduction, and thank you to the host.

2. Opening Prayer

3. Facilitator asks for two volunteers to take notes and explains what is expected.

4. Facilitator begins by asking one question at a time then waiting for the conversation to unfold.

5. Once all of the questions have been answered, the facilitator collects the notebooks from the note takers.

6. Close the meeting with prayer. Often small groups will remain chatting for after the formal portion of the meeting and the facilitator should listen to this informal conversation because it will continue the creation of the congregational story.

After each meeting, the workshop facilitator should transcribe the notes from each note taker into a narrative framework, if possible, using the questions as a guide to recreating the conversation. Once all of the meetings have been held, the facilitator should gather up each small group's narrative and compile them into a single narrative document that will seek to place all of the themes, issues and stories each group was creating into a single whole story.

Next, this single whole story will be printed in the congregation's newsletter, handed out during the next two to three week's worship or electronically sent to all members of the congregation. This will allow every member of the congregation to read what was said at each of the meetings and begin to sense the narrative being created. It will also allow stories not always heard by everyone in the congregation to be heard and to be understood as part of the whole congregation's story, rather than as the viewpoint of a faction or small group within the congregation. This will allow transparency to become part of the process without directly stating, "now we are going to be transparent," which often fails to become reality.

It is important to note that the congregation's governing board does not have editing power over this document, nor is permission from the governing board sought prior to communicating the narrative to the congregation. This will lend authenticity to the narrative being created, since it may include issues, concerns, or perspectives that have been ignored or silenced previously. Additionally, this burgeoning narrative should be included in sermons and discussions with the congregation over the course of the change and transition process and may be included in future newsletter articles.

The Second Workshop

The second workshop may be completed in one of two ways. First, it may be completed as an intensive one-day workshop at a local retreat facility or at another church that is nearby. This option encourages a maximum level of participation from the congregation because it is a one-day commitment. Young adults and young families find this option particularly attractive, since it allows them to participate without increasing a time commitment that will take them away from other Friday night or Saturday family activities. The facilitator should be aware of how many families with elementary children and youth are committed to school activities such as concerts or sports, since this will determine their ability to participate in this process and have their voices heard within the congregation. This is important for the encouragement of developing new leadership within the congregation, especially if young adults and young families are either not represented or lightly represented within the congregation's leadership structure.

In addition, this will lead directly into a conversation about developing new leaders for the congregation that is a critical component of a healthy and growing congregation.

Of course, if the congregation has a generally high level of commitment, it is possible to complete this second workshop through the second option of a two-day retreat format at a retreat center that is within a reasonable travel distance from the congregation's locale. The benefit of this option is that it will allow for some thinking and pondering time after the first workshop session that may lead to a more well-thought-out identity statement and higher quality brainstorming at the end of the second workshop session. Also, this option has the benefit of encouraging fellowship and conversations that may be helpful and instructive for the facilitator and his/her ministry with the congregation.

Whichever option is chosen for completing this second workshop, there are several key elements to it. The first is selecting a site away from the congregation's facility, so the trap of familiarity doesn't lead the participants into the usual paradigms of thought. The chosen site should have one large meeting space that can be arranged in a variety of ways and smaller meeting rooms for small group meetings. Sufficient breaks and meal times should be scheduled to allow for rest in the midst of the session. This is particularly important for the one-day intensive workshop.

Discouraging people to come and go during the session is important, since each element of the workshop will build upon the others and all elements are integral for comprehending the movement toward creating an identity statement. People who leave will not understand how the identity statement was formulated because they won't have participated in the flow of conversation and ideas leading to the statement and those coming later in the workshop will be entering a continuing conversation and will be unable to make constructive contributions to the identity statement. Indeed, the level of commitment by members of the congregation to attend this workshop will reveal more about the congregation than attending meetings or listening to congregational stories will often reveal.

In addition to the key elements stated above, the facilitator must be aware of the difference between an "identity" statement and a "mission" statement. Mission statements are usually vague lengthy statements aimed at speaking about intentions to do something and are often not used or referenced except in written communications or framed for display, then quickly forgotten. This often happens to corporate mission statements that may be familiar to many people within the congregation.

An identity statement is a one sentence, concrete, active-voice statement about the congregation's values and reason for existence. It is the lens through which they comprehend the world and through which they envision a future that will lead them to do particular actions. This difference encourages a congregation to think more deeply and creatively about themselves and aids in making the statement unique to this particular gathering of God's people. Additionally, this particularity leads them to do actions that are coherent with their identity. These are actions that prove the congregation is who it says it is.

If the congregation is in the interim between permanent pastors the clarity of the identity statement will encourage the congregation to seek a particular person for their next pastor who has a particular type of personality, particular gifts, skills and level of experience. This new pastor will become a resource and a member of the leadership team guiding the congregation to live into their thriving and sustainable future. This outcome is a direct refutation of the age old and outmoded attitude that "one-size" fits all or that the called pastor, who has all the answers, will direct the congregation where the pastor wants them to go in a top down fashion regardless of their sense of being a people with a particular story. In this current age, congregations are hungering for greater creativity and a stronger voice in discerning their future, particularly those with young adults and young families; creating an identity statement will address this hunger.

Also, the uniqueness of a particular congregation seeking a pastor will be evident in their congregational résumé that will be circulated through denominational matching services or to pastors seeking congregations to serve, since it will set them apart from congregations using the same tired language of mission statements that make every congregation sound the same while hiding their distinctiveness.

The Curriculum of the Second Workshop

One Day Intensive Workshop

Morning Session (2 Hours)

Learning Objectives

1. Learners will be empowered to share their stories and discover how these stories shape their identity. They will be encouraged to place their personal stories in the context of the biblical story, so that they might understand that their stories are woven in the biblical narrative as part of the holistic narrative of God's people.

The Workshop

Worship (see Appendix 1)

The Power of Narrative Workshop

1. Small Groups - Sharing stories and discovering how they shape us.

Each person shares one story from their life. After each story has been shared ask," How do the stories of our lives tell others about who we are?"

2. Small groups - Peters Projection Map vs. Mercator Map (see Appendix 1)

Break into small groups and give each group the Peters Projection Map vs. Mercator Map handout. Once the exercise is complete bring back the small groups into a large group to share and discuss answers to the handout.

Facilitator Note: You will want to introduce the maps by using the information from the book listed in the resource section of this workshop. It is better to give just a brief description of each map, so the groups will be able to be creative in the story telling of this exercise and not simply parroting back information you have given them. Also, you should be familiar with each map, so you will be able to help the groups answer the questions if they get stuck.

In addition, you will be leading part of the large group discussion by saying that there are a variety of maps of the world and each map is designed to have people see the world from a particular perspective.

For example; the Mercator Map was designed to be used in the 16th Century by ship navigators. However, it has been used as "the map of the world" by Western Europe and North America for centuries and has influenced and played a part in shaping our economic, political, and social ideas about the world.

In the same way, each person has their own personal map of the world- -the way we see and perceive the world around us that shapes our decisions, our ways of being and our choices. Even congregations have a map they use to define who they are and how they understand the world based upon the stories they tell about themselves, their geographic location, and their relationship to the local community. This leads to the next exercise.

2. Small Group Work -Where is your story in scripture?

Prepare this by telling the story of Ethiopian eunuch finding his story in the Isaiah passage he read.

a. What story in the Bible is important to you and why?

b. If participants do not identify themselves in a particular biblical story then ask, "Where do you see yourself in the Ethiopian eunuch story?

c. How has this biblical story shaped your life?

3. **Large Group Work** – "Power of Narrative" Power Point Presentation (Available on the Story Change Consultant web site)

5. Worship (See Appendix 1)

Afternoon Session (2 hours)

Learning Objectives

1. Learners will discover how the holistic narrative of God shapes their identity as a people and how identity leads to meaning for life. Also, how living based on identity and meaning leads to actions and choices that exhibit well-being and vitality.

2. Learners will create a new congregational identity statement as a response to God's call and gathering of this community of faith together and one that will include the past, present and future. This will be summarized in a one-sentence statement.

The Workshop

As people gather, have them write on the congregational timeline significant events in their lives as members of the congregation and significant events in the congregation's life.

Worship (see Appendix 1)

1. Small Group Work - Why is a narrative important for a congregation?

a. <u>Watership Down</u> – Telling a story that forms a community

Read "The Story of the Blessing of El-ahrairah" from *Watership Down, Part One, Chapter Six* before breaking into small groups to answer the following questions:

b. Ask, "What kind of a story is this?"

c. Ask, "Why is this story important to the rabbits?"

d. Ask, "How does this story shape the rabbits' identity?"

e. Each group comes back and shares their findings.

2. Small Group Work - Who do people say I am?

a. Read Luke 9:18

b. What are the names given to Jesus by people?

c. What other names is Jesus given?

1. Suffering servant from Isaiah

2. Jesus-God saves

3. Emmanuel - God with us

d. What do these names tell us about Jesus' identity and what Jesus does?

e. Each group comes back and shares their ideas.

3. Large Group Work - What are your names as a congregation?

    a. Christian

    b. Presbyterian (Or, other denominational identity)

    c. Name of the church

4. Large Group Work - Where do these names come from and why is that important?

    a. Christians-followers of Christ; imitators of Christ; ambassadors of Christ - Colossians 3:12-15

    b. If Presbyterians - Reformers coming from Switzerland (Calvin), Scotland (John Knox); if another denomination the historical roots of the denomination.

    c. History of church's name

5. Large Group Work - What story is our congregation's story?

    a. Read from 1 Thessalonians 4:1-11

    b. How does this story tell us who the Thessalonians are? How does it tell us their identity and purpose for life in the same way that the stories of Jesus' names tell us who he is and the stories of our names tell us who we are?

6. Small Group Work - How does the congregation's story fit into the biblical story?

How do our individual life stories connect to the congregational story and the biblical story? Each group comes back and shares their insights.

7. Craft a congregational identity statement based upon weaving the individual stories, the congregational story and the biblical story into one holistic story.

The facilitator will need to state the parameters for the identity statement (an and b below) without allowing for deviations from this format. Allowing longer, vague statements will render it useless going forward. The congregation will not realize this is true.

    a. Statement must be one sentence that is concrete, clear and avoids vague descriptors.

    b. Statement should begin with "We are" because it is about the congregation's identity, not about what they "will do" or "seek to do."

8. From identity to intentional living

This is the moment to ask, "How do we live the identity statement, so that what we do reflects who we say we are?" The facilitator will encourage the participants to answer the question by brainstorming possible answers.

9. Worship (see Appendix 1)

Two Day Retreat Workshop

Evening Session (1 Hour)

Learning Objectives

1. Learners will be empowered to share their stories and discover how these stories shape their identity. They will be encouraged to place their personal stories in the context of the biblical story, so that they might understand that their stories are connected to the biblical narrative as part of the holistic narrative of God's people.

The Workshop

Worship (see Appendix 1)

The Power of Narrative Workshop

   1. Small Groups - Sharing stories and discovering how they shape us.

   Each person shares one story from their life. After each story has been shared, ask, "How do the stories of our lives tell others about who we are?"

Morning Session (2 Hours)

Learning Objectives

1. Learners will be empowered to share their stories and discover how these stories shape their identity. They will be encouraged to place their personal stories in the context of the biblical story, so that they might understand that their stories are connected to the biblical narrative as part of the holistic narrative of God's people.

The Workshop

Worship (see Appendix1)

The Power of Narrative Workshop

1. **Small groups** - Peters Projection Map vs. Mercator Map Break into small groups and give each group the Peters Projection Map vs. Mercator Map handout. Once the exercise is complete, bring back the small groups into a large group to share and discuss answers to the handout.

Facilitator Note: You will want to introduce the maps by using the information from the book listed in the resource section of this workshop. It is better to give just a brief description of each map, so they will be able to be creative in the story telling of this exercise, not simply parroting back information you have given them. Also, you should be familiar enough with each map, so that you will be able to help the groups answer the questions if they get stuck.

In addition, you will be leading part of the large group discussion by saying that there are a variety of maps of the world and each map is designed to have people see the world from a particular perspective.

For example; the Mercator Map was designed to be used in the 16th Century by ship navigators. However, it has been used as "the map of the world" by Western Europe and North America for centuries and has influenced and played a part in shaping our economic, political, and social ideas about the world.

In the same way, each person has their own personal map of the world--the way we see and perceive the world around us that shapes our decisions, our ways of being and our choices. Even congregations have a map they use to define whom they are and how they understand the world based upon the stories they tell about themselves, their geographic location, and their relationship to the local community. This leads to the next exercise.

2. Small Group Work – Psalm 145 (10 minutes)

This assignment is the transition between sharing stories as defining whom we are, understanding that maps are visual stories defining our perspective on the world, and linking the biblical narrative to our life story. This assignment begins exploring how we use the biblical narrative, our personal stories and our perspective on the world to define our identity, defining the "why" of our existence.

a. Break the large group into their small groups.

b. Hand each person the exercise instruction sheet. (see Appendix 1)

c. Bring the groups back together and discuss their findings.

Ask, "What did you find in the psalm? What image was significant for you?"

d. Get back into your small groups and write a story about the people who might sing this psalm and base it solely on this psalm.

e. Each group reads their story.

2. Small Group Work -Where is your story?

Prepare this by telling the story of Ethiopian eunuch finding his story in the Isaiah passage he read. Then ask them to answer the following questions:

a. What story in the Bible is important to you and why?

b. If participants do not identify themselves in a particular biblical story then ask, "Where do you see yourself in the Ethiopian eunuch story?

c. How has this biblical story shaped your life?

3. Large Group Work - Power of Narrative Power Point Presentation (Available on Story Change Consultant web site)

5. Worship (see Appendix 1)

Afternoon Session (2 hours)

Learning Objectives

1. Learners will discover how the holistic narrative of God shapes their identity as a people and how identity leads to meaning for life. They will also explore how living from identity and meaning leads to actions and choices that exhibit well-being and vitality.

The Workshop

As people gather have them write on the congregational timeline significant events in their lives as members of the congregation and significant events in the congregation's life.

1. Worship (see Appendix 1)

2. Small Group Work - Why is a narrative important for a congregation?

>a. <u>Watership Down</u> – Telling a story that forms a community Read "The Story of the Blessing of El-ahrairah" from <u>Watership Down,</u> Part One, Chapter Six. Then ask the following questions:

>b. Ask, "What kind of a story is this?"

>c. Ask, "Why is this story important to the rabbits?"

>d. Ask, "How does this story shape the rabbits' identity?"

>e. Each group comes back shares their findings.

3. Small Group Work - Who do people say I am?

    a. Read Luke 9:18

    b. What are the names given to Jesus by people?

    c. What other names is Jesus given?

1. Suffering servant from Isaiah

2. Jesus-God saves

3. Emmanuel - God with us

    d. What do these names tell us about Jesus' identity and what Jesus does?

    e. Each group comes back and shares their ideas.

4. Large Group Work - What are our names as a congregation?

    a. Christian

    b. Presbyterian (Or, other denominational identity)

    c. Name of the church

5. Large Group Work - Where do these names come from and why is that important?

    a. Christians-followers of Christ; imitators of Christ; ambassadors of Christ - Colossians 3:12-15

    b. Presbyterians - Reformers coming from Switzerland (Calvin), Scotland (John Knox) (If another denomination what is the historical roots of the denomination)

    c. History of church's name

6. Large Group Work - What story is our congregation's story?

    a. Read from 1 Thessalonians 4:1-11

    b. How does this story speak about the Thessalonians

identity? How does it tell us their identity and purpose for life in the same way that the stories of Jesus' names tell us who he is and the story of our names tell us who we are?

7. Small Group Work - How does the congregation's story fit into the biblical story?

    a. How do our individual life stories connect to the congregational story and the biblical story?

    Each group comes back and shares their insights.

8. Worship (see Appendix 1)

Evening Session (1.5 Hours)

Learning Objectives

1. Learners will create a new congregational identity statement as a response to God's call and gathering of this community of faith together and one that will include the past, present and future. This will be summarized in a one-sentence statement.

The Workshop

1. Worship (see Appendix 1)

2. Craft a congregational identity statement based upon weaving the individual stories, the congregational story and the biblical story into one holistic story.

The facilitator will need to state the parameters for the identity statement (a and b below) without allowing for deviations from this format. Allowing longer, vague statements will render it useless going forward. The congregation will not realize this is true.

   a. Statement must be one sentence that is concrete, clear and avoids vague descriptors.

   b. Statement should begin with "We are" because it is about the congregation's identity, not about what they "will do" or "seek to do."

3. From identity to intentional living

This is the moment to ask, "How do we live the identity statement, so that what we do reflects who we say we are?" The facilitator will encourage participants to answer the question by brainstorming possible answers.

4. Worship (see Appendix 1)

Morning Session

Closing Worship (see Appendix 1)

The Logistics of the Second Workshop

Prior to beginning this workout session, the facilitator will need to have all of the following materials in hand (see appendix for map suppliers):

A large Mercator Map to post on a wall

A large Peter's Projection map to post on a wall

Postcards of the Peter's Projection map with colored dots on the back of each one

Four or five sheets of newsprint with short quotes written on them to be posted on a wall

All of the handouts for each workshop and order of worship for each worship

Materials to create a worship space such as candles, colored cloths, cross, incense

Either musicians, a cd player, or an iPod with speakers for music to accompany

congregational singing during worship

A computer and projector for the PowerPoint presentation

Markers, writing instruments, and Bibles.

Refreshments for breaks and food for continental breakfast and lunch (one-day intensive retreat)

Refreshments for breaks and foods for each of the meals (two-day retreat)

Post signs designating small group meeting spaces

The workshop begins in the large meeting space with chairs arranged in a circle, so everyone is able to see each other. The worship space is placed in the middle of the circle. As participants arrive they are handed a postcard of the Peter's Projection map with a colored dot on the back. The colored dot will be used to break the large group into small groups randomly put together through the use of the colored dots. Therefore, the colored dots should be mixed up in the large deck of postcards. Once the participants have a postcard, they are invited to read the quotes on the newsprint sheets posted throughout the large meeting room and to write their first reaction to the quote using one of the markers at each newsprint station. Once they have commented on all of the quotes, invite the participants to have refreshment and food until all the participants have arrived.

At the designated starting time, gather all participants into the large meeting room and invite them to find a place to sit, so they are part of the circle. Once all are seated proceed to welcome everyone, outline the activities for the day, and explain the meaning of the colored dots. Discourage participants from swapping colors to be with their friends, but to enjoy the randomness of their small group.

If doing the two-day workout, it will be helpful to post a schedule of beginning and ending times for each portion of the workshop. This can be simply when the workshop sessions begin and end for the evening session the day of arrival, the morning and afternoon and evening sessions for the day, and the morning session for the day of leaving.

Once all the questions have been answered, invite participants into worship. This begins the workshop.

The identity statement that is produced from this workshop session is printed in the bulletin each week, in the monthly newsletter, on the congregation's letterhead, and on the congregation's website, if they have a website. The pastor will use this in sermons when speaking about who the congregation is. All of these uses of the identity statement are designed to ingrain it in the congregation's memory. In addition, if the congregation is in the interim between permanent pastors this identity statement will complete the denominational Mission Information Form's section titled "mission statement," since the purpose of this portion of the change and transition process is designed to feed into that form. This is the form that is used to search for an installed pastor.

The Third Workshop

Very often the community context of a congregation becomes invisible like a familiar lamp sitting on an end table in the living room that no one notices anymore because it has faded into the background of our perceptions. I learned this lesson the hard way helping clients to report an insurance claim after a fire. Very often, the clients stared at the smoldering ashes without being able to remember what furniture was in the particular room or only remembered the furniture they had replaced years before. Congregations do the same with the communities within which they live. Often they fail to see what is currently happening in their community or can only see the community the way it was in a bygone era universally described as "the golden age."

However, communities are like living, breathing organisms, which are constantly changing and whose needs are changing as well. Thus, the focus of the third workshop is aimed at guiding the congregation to observe their community. The congregation will be guided to discern how their identity coupled with the congregation's passions to do ministries and missions flowing from that identity intersects with the needs of the community. The congregation will also evaluate their current ministries and missions to determine if they are consonant with both the congregational identity and the needs of the community. In addition, the congregation will learn how focusing on the health and peace of the community will help them to reclaim the call to embody Christ and lead them to their own well-being and peace in Christ.

This workshop begins by gathering members of the congregation together to study Jeremiah 29:1-11, 1 Corinthians 12-13, and the Hebrew word shalom.

Jeremiah 29:1-11 reads:

These are the words of the letter that the prophet Jeremiah sent from Jerusalem to the remaining elders among the exiles, and to the priests, the prophets, and all the people, whom Nebuchadnezzar had taken into exile from Jerusalem to Babylon. ² This was after King Jeconiah, and the queen mother, the court officials, the leaders of Judah and Jerusalem, the artisans, and the smiths had departed from Jerusalem. ³ The letter was sent by the hand of Elasah son of Shaphan and Gemariah son of Hilkiah, whom King Zedekiah of Judah sent to Babylon to King Nebuchadnezzar of Babylon. It said: ⁴ Thus says the LORD of hosts, the God of Israel, to all the exiles whom I have sent into exile from Jerusalem to Babylon: ⁵ Build houses and live in them; plant gardens and eat what they produce. ⁶ Take wives and have sons and daughters; take wives for your sons, and give your daughters in marriage, that they may bear sons and daughters; multiply there, and do not decrease. ⁷ But seek the welfare of the city where I have sent you into exile, and pray to the LORD on its behalf, for in its welfare you will find your welfare. ⁸ For thus says the LORD of hosts, the God of Israel: Do not let the prophets and the diviners who are among you deceive you, and do not listen to the dreams that they dream,[d] ⁹for it is a lie that they are prophesying to you in my name; I did not send them, says the LORD.*¹⁰For thus says the* LORD: *Only when Babylon's seventy years are completed will I visit you, and I will fulfill to you my promise and bring you back to this place.¹¹ For surely I know the plans I have for you, says the* LORD, *plans for your welfare and not for harm, to give you a future with hope.* (NRSV)

The focus for Jeremiah 29:1-11 is to hear God's words promising well-being, health, peace and homecoming to Israel even as Israel dwells in exile. Yet, these promises come with the obligation to be attentive to God and not to false prophets. These promises also ask the people of Israel to be attentive to Israel's obligation to seek the well-being, the health, and the peace of the community within which they dwell. God ties the exiles' future to the present and the future of the community where God has sent them to live. The key word in this study is the Hebrew word "shalom," usually translated as "welfare," which can also be translated as "health," "well-being," "wholeness," and "peace." Therefore, the word study of shalom becomes an important aspect for understanding the portion of scripture under study in Jeremiah.

The study of 1 Corinthian:12-13 is important for considering the diverse gifts of the congregation as well as the diverse needs of the community. I have discovered over the years of my ministry that too often, congregations define mission as food pantries, clothes closets, home repair or renovation projects, leaf raking, and a number of other more visible projects. Seldom do congregations look beyond those obvious needs to focus on deeper needs such as reading partners for children; tutoring for all ages; vocational discernment for middle school students, high school students, and adults needing to transition from one vocation to the next; sustainable vegetable gardening; starting a local business and any number of projects that will seek to solve the systemic issues keeping people hungry, naked, unhealthy, living in violent homes or cities and in substandard housing.

Thus, the 1 Corinthians study will start a conversation about the diversity of gifts God gives to each one of us and how we might use those gifts to bring well-being, health and peace to the community by connecting gifts, abilities or talents of the congregation to the needs of the community.

Critical to both of these bible studies is observing what is happening in the community and what is visible in the community when people walk through the streets and neighborhoods or ride down roads in rural communities. Participants will write notes about what they see without interpreting the meaning of what they see, gather statistical information that will add to the congregation's knowledge and understanding of their community, and interview community leaders about the needs of the community. Once the Bible studies have been completed, the congregation is given a choice either to become part of the walking and driving observer group, to become part of the statistical information research group or to become part of interview community leaders group.

The walking and driving observer group will divide the community between them with some walking neighborhoods and others driving the wider boundaries of the community. In each case the goal is to note what is observed and bring the observations back to the larger congregational group. The key to this is observation only, while not evaluating or interpreting the observations until the larger congregational group meeting.

At the same time that the walking and driving observers are engaged in their tasks, the statistical information research group will perform a demographic study of the community by gathering key Census Bureau statistics regarding community population breakdown by age, income, ethnicity, education, housing type, living wage, vocation, and religious affiliation, using a form provided to them.

The interviewing group will contact people in the community who see the community from diverse perspectives and ask them questions about crime, the impact of immigration, school dropout rates, unemployment, and child care. Some of the people interviewed might be the head of law enforcement, Catholic Charities Director, School Superintendent, Rural and Migrant Ministries, free health clinics, or the Literacy Program Director. The persons to be interviewed will differ for each community and must be decided by congregational members living in the community.

The observation group, the statistical information research group and the interviewing group will aid the congregation in reframing their knowledge about the community. This knowledge might empower them to see how diverse issues can be interrelated, and through their connections, positively or negatively impact the health, well-being, wholeness or peace of the community. For example, a high preponderance of rental property in a community with a high number of households living below the poverty level combined with high number of payday loan and furniture rental companies may suggest the need for ministries serving the needs of poor families. These ministries might include providing resources aimed at family stability, food pantries, building safe and affordable owner occupied homes, or even a need for cooperative financial institution with a program of micro-lending, so local people may be able to create businesses that provide income and jobs for members of the community.

These connections are made once all of the groups have completed their work and a follow-up meeting is scheduled to discuss the findings of each group. The following questions provide an avenue to hear each group's report and begin the discussion of what these findings mean for the community;

1. What significant changes have happened in your community in the last (x) years?

2. How have these changes influenced or impacted the congregation?

3. How many of the homes in the community are primarily rental and how many are owner-occupied? What is the percentage of people in your community living below the poverty level?

4. What are the education and income levels within the community? What is the high school dropout rate and what is the unemployment rate? What is it for each ethnic/racial group in the community?

5. What did you observe?

6. What community issues did the interviews uncover?

7. Who in your community is addressing those issues and what is your relationship with them?

The facilitator should be noting the community needs identified during the discussion on a large board or newsprint paper, so that a list emerges at the end of the discussion. Next, the facilitator leads a brief discussion about the list to discern if it appears complete at that moment. When the congregation agrees it is complete, the facilitator then leads a brainstorming session to create a list of mission activities that will address the identified community needs. Once the brainstorming has been completed, then the facilitator asks the congregation, "Which of these mission activities fits who you say you are?" Here is where the needs of the community intersect with the identity of the congregation as the congregation begins new ministries that reflect their identity. This where their "why"—their values, beliefs and identity—are proved by what the congregation does. This also marks the start of a new culture within the congregation. The next step is for the facilitator to ask, "Who has the passion, the energy and imagination to do the identified mission activity to meet a community need?"

The reason for this question is that passion, energy and imagination will provide the basis for a person to act and to find joy and perseverance in doing the mission they choose to do. Acting from duty or obligation will often fail to instill joy and perseverance, especially when creating a new mission requiring collaboration with other people and organizations within a community.

In addition, the identity of the congregation and the needs of the community become dual evaluation tools for the congregation and congregational leadership to review missions and other congregational activities to discern which need to be reframed, redeveloped or ended because they no longer meet a community need or are no longer reflective of the congregation's identity.

Again, the facilitator will want to create a report discussing the outcome of this portion of the narrative process, so everyone has a written account of the decisions that have been made and the reasoning behind those decisions. The report will also explain the new ministries that will be starting, their tie to a particular community need, and the way the congregation lives into its identity through the new mission.

The Final Step in Workshop Process (optional)

If the congregation is in the interim between "called" or permanent pastors, the final step in the workshop series will be to have the congregation complete the "Pastoral Competencies and Leadership Style" questionnaire. This questionnaire was developed by adapting the Meyers-Briggs Type Indicator and the current Presbyterian Church pastoral skills list with the interpretation of the results created by utilizing Roy M. Oswald and Otto Kroeger's work "Personality Type and Religious Leadership," which is an excellent resource for suggesting strengths and challenges for each personality type. Other Christian denominations and faith traditions may adapt this questionnaire to fit within the particularities of their pastoral leader selection process.

Too often, calling a pastor resembles a barbershop where the barber has an empty chair and is yelling, "Next." Thus, a need exists to discern the leadership and pastoral ministry skills and gifts a congregation needs if it is going to intentionally live toward the future God is calling the congregation to embrace. I would suggest that this discernment comes during the first three steps in this process and is brought to fruition here in this step of the process when the congregation reviews the following list of diverse skills and chooses those which will be critical for the pastor to have, so she/he will be equipped to lead the congregation into their future.

Beyond the necessary level of experience and expertise, these skills and gifts will aid the congregation in calling a pastor. They will be able to evaluate each person's suitability based upon their pastoral skills, personal engagement and understanding of where the congregation is journeying next as well as how well the pastoral candidate sees themselves fitting into that journey. For the congregation, this moves the call process beyond whether the congregation "likes" the way the person preaches or their level of experience to whether this candidate will empower them for the ministry they are seeking to do. This approach enables the congregation to seek the person capable of guiding them to health and vitality and the person able to articulate the congregation's vision for the future as a ministry glorifying God.

For the pastoral candidate, this moves the call process toward a positive discernment about whether God is calling them to serve the particular congregation because their pastoral skills and gifts are congruent with the needs of the particular congregation.

In addition, the skills and leadership styles, like the identity statement and missions the congregation will be doing, are designed to be used in completing the Ministry Information Form if Presbyterian (U.S.A.) and may be adapted for other denominations and faith traditions to use in their particular process. For this reason, also, preparing a report of the questionnaire outcome is important. This report should indicate what the particular leadership style's strengths and weaknesses will be, so the congregation has a fuller understanding about the person they are seeking to call.

The Logistics for the Optional Final Step

The facilitator distributes the questionnaire to the congregation in printed format or in electronic format guided by the communication methods utilized in the workshops. Members of the congregation are encouraged to complete the questionnaire and return it to the facilitator. None of the congregational leaders should be included in the gathering or scoring of the questionnaire, so that the integrity of the scoring and interpretative aspects of this step in the process may be maintained.

Once the facilitator has the completed questionnaires, the facilitator then adds up the various choices to determine the congregation's preferences for the personality type and the skills or competencies needed in the next pastor or pastoral leader. The facilitator will then interpret the results based upon the congregation's identity and missions by pointing out the strengths and challenges of the person they are seeking as well as whether the person sought will be the pastoral leader the congregation needs to partner with them in living into their vision of their future. This report, also, should suggest how the congregation may need to adjust their ways of doing administrative tasks or other practices, so the person they call to be the pastor may flourish in their midst. Additionally, the report might suggest possible questions the committee doing the pastoral interviews might want to ask of each candidate.

Again, the report the facilitator creates for this step should be sent to every member of the congregation, so everyone has the same information. This creates transparency and integrity for the process.

Pastoral Competencies and Leadership Style Questionnaire

These two lists present competencies for pastoral ministry and leadership styles. You will select the leadership style first then look at the competency list and discern which ten are most important for the associate pastor to possess, so she or he will be empowered to lead you with intentionality into your future. When you are considering these various choices it is helpful to keep in mind your identity statement, the ministries in which you want the associate pastor to engage as a resource person and as part of the leadership team, and the way this person will complement Rev. Bob Spratt both in leadership style and pastoral competencies.

Leadership Styles

Select one from each pair of the following style indicators.

I.

Introvert – A person who enjoys people, but who needs time alone to "recharge."

This is a person who is a good listener and who enjoys peace and quiet.

Extrovert – This is a person who is easily engaged by friends and strangers alike and gains energy by working with groups of people to generate ideas.

II.

Judging – Self-disciplined and purposeful. Decisive, plans ahead, get things done, organized and scheduled.

Perceiving – Flexible and adaptable. Curious, seeks out experience, responds to situations, adapts and changes on the go.

III.

Sensing – Perceives with the five senses and seeks practical and factual details, down to earth and in the present moment, sensible, concrete, meticulous and systematic. Wants to actively do ministry.

Intuitive – Aware of patterns and meanings, possibilities for the future, looking for the big picture, change-oriented and imaginative. Relies on hunches and is spontaneous, perceives with memory and associations.

IV

Thinking – Uses logical analysis and objective and impersonal criteria. Is firm-minded, analytical, relates to things, ideas, and concepts.

Feeling – Weighs human values and motives both their own and others, values warm relationships and is trusting, persuasive, tactful, relates well to people, teacher.

LEADERSHIP COMPETENCIES

THEOLOGICAL/SPIRITUAL INTERPRETER

Compassionate – having the ability to suffer with others; being motivated by others pain and is called into action as advocate; is motivated by caring for others while concurrently keeping the organizational goals clearly in focus.	**Hopeful** – maintains stability in the moment and hope for the future; provides direction, guidance, and faith when describing basic needs; and helps followers to see a way through chaos and complexity.
Preaching and Worship Leadership: Is a consistently effective preacher and worship leader; is able to inspire from the pulpit; communicates a clear and consistent message through sermons that are carefully prepared and artfully delivered; projects the identity and character of the congregation through worship leadership presence.	**Spiritual Maturity:** Shows strong personal depth and spiritual grounding; demonstrates integrity by walking the talk and by responding with faithfulness of purpose; is seen by others as trustworthy and authentic; nurtures a rich spiritual life; seeks the wisdom and guidance of appropriate mentors; is able to articulate a clear and consistent theology.
Lifelong Learner – individuals who use every experience in life as a potential tool for growth; one who pursues	**Teacher** – creates learning environments where students are active participants as individuals and as members of collaborative groups; designs lesson plans that

continuing education; and those who build on strengths and seek assistance to improve weaknesses.	teach concepts, facts, and theology; effectively uses multiple learning tools to reach a wide variety of learners; revises instructional strategies based upon ministry/organization context.

COMMUNICATION

Communicator - Advances the abilities of individuals and the organizations through active listening supported with meaningful oral and written presentation of information.	**Bilingual** – having the ability to use two languages, especially with equal or nearly equal fluency; able to use multiple languages in communication.
Public Communicator - Demonstrates a comfortable ease when speaking in a variety of settings (both small and large groups); is effective at addressing a variety of topics; can get messages across with the desired effect.	**Media Communicator:** Has experience developing materials for a variety of written or multimedia forms of communications (print, Internet-based, social media, etc.)
Technologically Savvy - the ability to navigate successfully the world of technology using software, blogging, multi-	

media, and websites as tools for ministry.	

ORGANIZATIONAL LEADERSHIP

Advisor – an individual others turn to for counsel and guidance; provides coaching; expertise for congregations or other organizations.	**Change Agent** – having the ability to lead the change process successfully; anchoring the change in the congregation's/organization's vision and mission.
Contextualization – the ability to assess accurately the context, environment, history, relationships and uniqueness of a congregation or organization.	**Culturally Proficient** – having solid understanding of the norms, values and common behaviors of various peoples, including direct experience working in multiple cultural and cross-cultural settings.
Externally Aware - identifies and keeps informed of the polity of the church and/or the organization; maintains current with laws, regulations, policies, procedures, trends, and developments both internally and in the larger society.	**Entrepreneurial** - leaders that are creative in using resources; identifies opportunities to develop; is willing to take risks, initiates actions that involve a deliberate risk to achieve a recognized benefit or advantage.

	Risk Taker – persons with the ability to take appropriate risk to accomplish needed goals; one who thinks outside the box and who is not afraid of challenging the status-quo.		**Task Manager** - Assures that effective controls are developed and maintained to ensure the integrity of the organization; holds self and others accountable for rules and responsibilities; can be relied upon to ensure that projects within areas of specific responsibility are completed in a timely manner and within budget; and monitors and evaluates plans, focuses on results and measuring attainment of outcomes.
	Willingness to Engage Conflict: Steps up to conflicts, seeing them as opportunities; reads situations quickly; good at focused listening; can identify common ground and elicit cooperation from others in crafting mutual solutions.		**Decision Making:** Makes effective decisions, balancing analysis, wisdom, experience, and judgment; is aware of the long term implications of choices made; is generally regarded as offering solutions and suggestions that are correct and effective.
	Organizational Agility: Is astute about how congregations and/or organizations work; knows how to get things done through formal and informal channels; understands the importance of supporting good policy, practice, and procedure; appreciates the power in the culture		**Strategy and Vision:** Sees ahead clearly, keeping focused on the larger picture; can anticipate future consequences and trends accurately; is future oriented; casts a compelling and inspired vision for a preferred future; sees possibility; crafts breakthrough strategies.

of a congregation; is politically savvy.		
Financial Manager – deliver results by maximizing organizational effectiveness and sustainability through the best use of available financial resources; allocates and manages finances transparently; implements strategies to achieve operational efficiencies and value for money; puts in place rigorous and comprehensive financial accountability systems.		**Funds Developer** – maintains the ability to solicit donations used to fund the budget of the organization; effectively expresses the needs for funds to potential donors; responsible for adding new potential donors to the organization's contact list; prepares statement of planned activities and enlists support for mission initiatives.
Collaboration: Has a natural orientation toward getting people to work together; shares wins and successes; fosters open dialogue; lets people finish and be responsible for their work; creates strong feelings of belonging among group members; is a good judge of talent and can accurately assess the strengths and limitations of others.		

INTERPERSONAL ENGAGEMENT	
Interpersonal Engagement - Displays a consistent ability to build solid relationships of trust and respect inside and outside of the organization; engage people, organizations, and partners in developing goals, executing plans, and delivering results; use negotiation skills and adaptability to encourage recognition of joint concerns, collaboration, and to influence the success of outcomes.	**Bridge Builder** – possessing a certain responsibility for the unity of the congregation and or organization; works to connect people of different cultures, worldviews, and theological positions.
Motivator - Creates and sustains an organizational culture which permits others to provide the quality of service essential to high performance. Enables others to acquire the tools and support they need to perform well; and influences others toward a spirit of service and meaningful contributions to mission accomplishment.	**Personal Resilience:** Learns from adversity and failure; picks up on the need to change personal, interpersonal, and leadership behaviors; deals well with ambiguity; copes effectively with change; can decide and act without having the total picture; comfortably handles risk and uncertainty; seeks feedback; expresses personal regret when appropriate

Initiative: Demonstrates ambition is highly motivated; is action oriented and full of energy for things seen as challenging; seizes opportunity; pushes self and others to achieve desired results.	**Flexibility** - Adapts behavior and work methods in response to new information, changing conditions, unexpected obstacles, or ambiguity; remains open to new ideas and approaches; and works concurrently on related and conflicting priorities without losing focus or attention.
Self Differentiation: Demonstrates strong and appropriate personal boundaries in relationships; has a healthy appreciation of self, without being egotistical; is emotionally mature; can maintain a less- anxious presence in the midst of turmoil; is not overly dependent upon outside affirmation; works to build a strong personal support system.	

The Complementary Actions

The complementary actions of creating a new identity and creating worship to tell the story of God and God's people each week, each month and each season within the context of the communal meta-narrative of the Bible and the Christian calendar is only one portion of the congregation's journey through the forest of change and transition. The other portion of the journey are complementary actions of new ministries focused on community needs that reflect the congregation's new identity and Christian education classes for all ages, fellowship activities and congregational administrative policies and procedures. All of these complementary actions are designed to be integrated, so the congregation is one whole and holistic community of God's people taking a journey through the forest of change and transition, which will take seven to ten years to complete.

During this journey, the congregation's administrative structure or polity of governing boards, committees, task forces or teams will need to reframe their purposes and tasks in reference to the new congregational identity. The governing board of the congregation will want to evaluate how its work supports the congregation's identity by having each committee, task force and team write out a brief purpose statement that describes how the tasks delegated to it support the congregation living into its identity. These purpose statements should use clear, concise language, avoiding the vague language of mission statements that sound nice, but say nothing about what they actually do. Additionally, each committee, task force and team should list below the purpose statement the tasks delegated to it by the governing board, the ways each committee, task force and team collaborates with each other, and what, if any, budget items or special funds are under their authority to use in support of the congregation's identity and ministry to the congregation and its ministry to the community within which it dwells and the world.

All of these purpose statements as well as all congregational policies and procedures should be gathered together into an operating manual, so each member of the governing board, the committees, task force and teams will have a copy for their use. A copy should be made available in the congregation's administrative office for the congregation to read and reference when questions arise.

Also, the governing board should review its policies and procedures paying particular attention to its annual operating budget to assure that all are congruent with congregation's new identity, making clear that every action the congregation takes is based upon who the congregation declares it is as it walks the talk.

Completing these administrative actions will deepen the congregation's commitment and acceptance of their new identity, since it will permeate everything the congregation does down to the details of how it spends its money through the budget and the way it organizes itself to do ministry and mission.

Coupled with these administrative actions is the creation of complementary Christian Education classes or programs. Christian education needs to be broad-based, with a strong focus on Bible studies for adults, children and youth. This is vital to a congregation since, as George Stroup has pointed out, one of the reasons for the crisis in Christian identity is biblical illiteracy (21-38). In addition, if the biblical narrative ceases to be foundational for congregations, Stroup wonders whether those congregations can "be said to be Christian" (252). Early on in the journey through the forest of change and transition, a Bible study of the psalms using Walter Brueggemann's schema of orientation, disorientation and re-orientation may be useful to teach the congregation the language of lament. They will become able to articulate their own grief or their own disorientation and teach the congregation the way to see how new beginnings do flow out from endings, reinforcing the notions that endings contain within them the seeds of new life.

In addition, using the biblical narrative for leadership training of Elders and Deacons is a powerful way to re-claim the biblical story as our story. This is clear when studying Jesus teaching his disciples to be leaders over their three years of following after him, his final teaching before he ascends and the way the apostles taught and empowered others to be leaders in the early years of the church. This is, of course, a way to teach about imitating Christ in our life together which is one more way to prompt the congregation to go back to the biblical story to see how this works in the context of the 1st Century and how it looks in the 21st Century. For example, if the congregation closely reads the Gospel According to Mark it will discover an emphasis on the three fold way of discipleship of denying self, meaning to focus on living according to God's will for humanity and creation; picking up a cross, meaning to be willing to voluntarily work for restorative justice, an end to oppression and violence in all its forms while working for the well-being of every person even at the risk of one's own suffering; and to follow Jesus, meaning using Jesus as the model for denying self and picking up a cross and as the model of obedience to God and the self-giving love that encourages each person to fully be the person God created them to be.

Another aspect of education may be developing small groups to explore the diversity of prayer practices as a way toward an authentic spirituality. Small groups may study the variety of prayer traditions such as the labyrinth, the Benedictine Rule, and Lectio Divina. They may also study Christian mystics such as Teresa of Avila, John of the Cross and Thomas Merton. Small groups may, in addition, want to attend conferences about spirituality and spiritual practices, particularly those with classes about healing through the power of narrative such as the work being done through the Soul Repair Center at Brite Divinity School with veterans of war and the work of Lewis

Mehl-Madonna, who has used narrative to heal the minds of persons with mental illness.

Using the power of narrative in this way reinforces the ability of narrative to be flexible, multi-layered and open to reinterpretation by the storyteller through gestures and shifts in vocal emphasis. In addition, we are reminded that narratives connect us to our families and our communities, so we know who we are and we know how to live in the world. As G. Sherwood wrote, "Story is comprised of experiences that are significant to the person, that define who one is. People connect through shared story in a powerful interaction that communicates relationships, transmits culture, socializes a new generation and communicates expectations. Reflections on story help us understand how to live and discover meaning" (Sherwood 2000). Narratives also create realty by weaving together past, present and future into a holistic story that is open ended enough to allow the narrative to be re-interpreted when life changes. As Stephen Crites states, "stories give qualitative substance to the form of experience because experience itself is a story" (72).

Finally, planning fellowship activities with attention paid to how those activities will reveal or will promote the congregation's identity deepens the cultural impact of the new identity in the same way that family meal times become the vehicle for creating each family member's identity through the telling of family stories, enacting rituals such as saying grace or who gets fed first, and even through the food that is served, and whether the table is round or rectangular.

The use of complementary actions to ensure the congregation's new identity permeates every aspect of congregational life, highlights the importance of intentionality and transparency in the practice of weaving narratives for a thriving, healthy, sustainable congregation. It is also the outcome of leading a congregation through the forest of change and transition by adapting John P. Kotter's process of change, being mindful of the deep emotional response to alterations in the material life circumstances of a congregation and the power of narrative, specifically the biblical narrative, to shape identity and meaning for the congregation.

Indeed, attentiveness to intentionality and transparency has been critical to the practice of leading congregations through the forest of change and transition by weaving narratives with the congregations I served, whether as an installed pastor called to lead congregations through planned change, an interim pastor leading congregations through the time between permanent pastors or as a consultant working with congregations on mission studies.

Just as identity and meaningfulness permeate the congregation's life, so too will intentionality and transparency permeate the congregation's life during the long journey toward a healthy, thriving and sustainable future.

Chapter 7

New Life Begins: Living Why to Thrive

So, when does the new beginning start? When does the congregation know it is thriving and healthy and on the path to a future that is sustainable? Will it be like turning the key in the ignition and hearing the engine roar to life or like flipping a switch and having light chase away the darkness in a room? While it would be wonderful and easy if one of those examples above described the reality of a congregation moving from an ending through the forest of change and transition to reach the destination of their future, it is more likely that the congregation will discover one day that they are healthier and have the energy of thriving without ever knowing precisely the exact time and day when it happened.

New beginnings start with an inner realignment of passion and energy which becomes a powerful self-motivating force rather than, as William Bridges writes, with some external affirmation. It is the realization that congregational life, like our individual lives, is not linear. Nor, does it conform to an analytical bell curve of congregational life stages designed to plot out when the congregation has moved beyond its useful life, like a battery, and when it might have time to regenerate back to a younger version of itself. Instead, a congregation's life is more like a spiral laid on its side showing where the congregation has been without predetermining where the next turn of the spiral will occur nor how large the spiral will actually be.

That is not to say that there won't be moments of doubt and anxiousness when a congregation does not sense that it is moving toward a rich future and moves back to familiar routines, processes and programs that seemed to work in the "good old days." However, when those moments arise congregational leaders will want to turn to the story in the Book of Numbers about the day the Hebrews were in the wilderness and were just outside the land God promised to them. Moses sent some spies to check out this land God promised to give to them. After they had done their work, the spies came back and reported what they saw and what they experienced. Of course, the majority of the spies told tales of giants and insurmountable obstacles that would doom the Hebrews if they tried to step even one foot into this land. It would be better they said, for the Hebrews to go back to Egypt and the life they had there. The minority report from two spies painted a much different picture. They boldly said the land was wonderful and filled with goodness. The Hebrews had a choice to make. Go back to what was familiar or go forward into the unknown land. The Hebrews chose to believe the majority report. The result of this choice was that the Hebrews wandered in the wilderness for the next forty years.

This story reminds congregations that risk is part of any new beginning, while trying to live in the past will only keep them wandering around in the wilderness. Or as Bridges points out, "no new time of life is possible without the death of the old lifetime. To gain, you must first give up" what is old (152). In addition, sometimes we have to be reminded that just because the majority believes something to be true does not always mean that it is true. The challenge to willingly leave behind a past that no longer is life nourishing, healthy or thriving means re-creating the stories congregations have told to define themselves to illuminate a new identity yielding new meaning and purpose for their lives. A new identity and purpose leading to a healthy and thriving future that can be sustained because the new stories the congregation tells are richer and run deeper within the lives and among the lives of the people of the congregation.

Stories weaving together the lives of the people into one whole congregational story, which is connected to the narrative of all God's people.

Appendix 1

Workshop Resources

Opening Worship for One Day and Two Day Retreats

Gathering Music (Choose music to set the tone for the workshop)

Opening responses

The world belongs to God
The earth and all its people.
How good it is, how wonderful,
To live together in unity.
Love and faith come together,
Justice and peace join hands
If Christ's disciples keep silent,
These stones would shout aloud.
Open our lips, O God,
And our mouths shall proclaim your works.

Prayer

O God, who gave to your servant Columba the gifts of courage, faith, and cheerfulness,
and sent people forth from Iona to carry the word of your gospel to every creature;
grant, we pray, a like spirit to this your church, even at this present time.
Further in all things the purpose of our community that hidden things may be revealed to us, and new ways found to touch the hearts of all. Amen.

Psalm 145

Silence

Sung Taizé Prayer "In God Alone"

Blessing

Worship is adapted from Iona Community from the *Iona Abbey Worship book*, Published by Wild Goose Publications, Iona Community, Unit 16, Six Harmony Row, Glasgow, Scotland.

Maps for the Peters Projection Map vs Mercator Map Exercise

The source for maps and postcards is: ODT, P.O. Box 134 Amherst, MA 01004 and on the web at www.odt.org

The Promise of Narrative Change

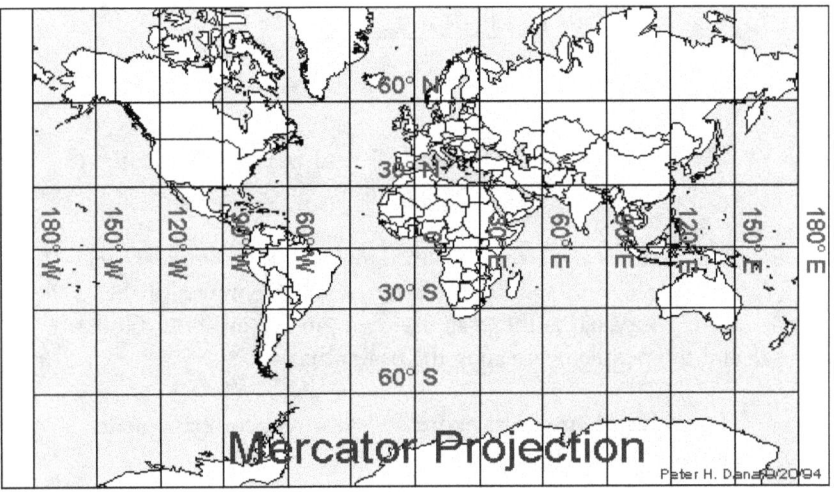

Peters Projection Map vs. Mercator Map Handout

1. What is similar about the maps?

2. What is different about the maps?

3. The Mapmakers' story

Blue Group: write a two-paragraph story about the people who created the Mercator map. In your story, tell whom the people are, how they use this map and their understanding of the world based solely on this map.

Green Group: write a two-paragraph story about the people who created the Peters Projection map. In your story, tell whom the people are, how they use this map and their understanding of the world based solely on this map.

Psalm of Orientation Handout - <u>This is a small group exercise for Two Day Retreat Workshop</u>

Psalm 145

1. Each person in the group will read psalm 145 silently. Then, answer the following questions:

This psalm is an acrostic psalm. This means the writer starts each verse with a different letter of the Hebrew alphabet from a-z. What is the psalmist trying to tell us about God and the people by creating the psalm this way?

How does the psalmist express God's free, compassionate and unlimited self-giving?

Where does the psalmist find God's self-giving in daily life?

How does this psalm orient us to life; our relationship with God and our relationship with each other?

Based on this psalm and other psalms of orientation, is there a part of life that is not sacred?

Worship for the end of the first Workshop Session

Opening responses

Jesus says, "I am the Way for you."
And so we come to follow Christ.
Jesus says, "I am the Truth for you."
And so we come to dwell in the light.
Jesus says, "I am the Life for you."
And so we come, leaving behind all else to which we cling.

Scripture Joshua 24: 14 -18

Invitation to commitment

What commitment will you make to God in the silence that follows?

Silence

Affirmation of Commitment

We are not alone; we live in God's world
We believe in God, who has created and is creating, who has come in Jesus, the
Word made flesh, to reconcile and make new, who works in us and others by the
Holy Spirit. We trust in God. We are called to be the church, to celebrate God's
presence, to live with respect in creation, to love and serve others, to seek justice
and resist evil, to proclaim Jesus crucified and risen, our hope. In life, in death, in
life beyond death God is with us. We are not alone. Thanks be to God. Amen.

Closing

Look at your hands; see the touch and the tenderness,
God's own for the world.

Look at your feet; see the path and the direction,
God's own for the world.

Look at your heart; see the fire and the love,
God's own for the world.

Look at the cross; see God's Son and our Savior,
God's own for the world.

This is God's world,
God's own for the world.

Blessing

May Christ's peace be with you all. Amen.

Worship for Afternoon Workshop Session

Gathering Music (U2- "40")

Opening Responses

God of all grace
Silence from whom our words come;
Questioner from whom our questions arise;
Lover of whom all our loves are hints;
Disturber in whom alone we find our rest;
Mystery in whose depths we find healing and our lives;
Enfold us now in your presence; restore to us your peace;
Renew us through your power; and ground us in your grace.

Silence

Prayer

Lord, You who gave bread to Moses and the Israelites while they traveled in the desert, come now, and bless the gifts of food which You give to us this day. As our food gives up its life for us, may we follow that pattern of self-surrender for each other. May we be life to one another. With grateful hearts we pray in Christ's name. Amen.

Luke 9:18

Silence

Colossians 3:12-15

Silence

Blessing

The opening response was adapted from Ted Loder's "Ground Me in Your Grace" from *Guerrillas of Grace: Prayers for the Battle* (Philadelphia: Innisfree Press, Inc. 1984)

The closing worship of the first session and this worship were adapted from Iona Community from the *Iona Abbey Worship book*, Published by Wild Goose Publications, Iona Community, Unit 16, Six Harmony Row, Glasgow, Scotland.

Worship to conclude Afternoon Session of Two Day Retreat

Call to Worship

Jesus is the light of the world.
The light no darkness can overcome.
Stay with us, Lord, for it is evening,
and the day is nearly over.
Let your light scatter the darkness
and illumine our way.

Reading Genesis 32:25-28

Silent Reflection

Reading Matthew 1:20-23

Silent Reflection

Closing Prayer

Benediction

Worship for Evening Session of Two Day Retreat

Gathering Music (Gregorian Chant with incense)

We enter worship in silence

Opening Responses

Loving God longs for a relationship with us.
Our Creator wants to satisfy our longings,
Hold us close and be there for us right when we call.
Our God whispers to us how wonderfully unique we all are
We are fearfully and wonderfully we are made.

Sung Taizé Prayer "Come and Fill Our Hearts"

Silence

Isaiah 43:18-19

Silence

We leave in silence when we are ready to begin our work together.

Worship to conclude Evening Session of Two Day Retreat

Call to Worship

Blessed is one whose help is the God of Rebekah and Jacob
Who made heaven and earth, the sea, and all that is in them.
Who keeps faith forever
Who executes justice for the oppressed.
Who gives food to the hungry
The Lord sets the prisoners free and opens the eyes of the blind.
The Lord lifts up those who are bowed down and loves the righteous.
The Lord watches over the sojourners,
And upholds the widow and the orphan. Come, we worship the Lord.

Prayer

Reading Psalm 121

Silent Reflection

Reading Matthew 5:1-16

Silent Reflection

Prayer of Discipleship

I am only one
But I am one!
I cannot do everything.
But I can do something!
And what I can do,
By the grace of God, I will do.

As we go forth in the world, may God guide us in being a blessing to our neighbors.

Benediction

Worship is adapted from Taizé *Worship Feast* and The Iona Community from *Iona Abbey Worship Book*, published by Wild Goose Publications, Iona Community
Unit 16, Six Harmony Row, Glasgow, Scotland.

Closing Worship for One Day and Two Day Retreat Workshops

Gathering Music (Gregorian Chant)

We enter in silence

Opening Responses

Let the light fall warm and red on the rock,
Let the birds sing their evening song
And let God's people find rest.
Let the tools be stored away,
Let the work be over and done
And let God's people find rest.

Let the flowers close and stars appear,
Let hearts be glad and minds be calm,
And let God's people find rest.

Silence

Sung Taizé Prayer "In God Alone"

Silence

Genesis 12:1-3

Silence

Visual Prayer with Gregorian chant (These are photographs of creation projected on a wall for all to see)

When you discern it is time to go home, do so with this blessing,

May the Lord bless you and keep you,

May the Lord be kind and gracious to you,
May the Lord look upon you with favor,
And grant you peace. Amen.

Worship is adapted from Taizé and from The Iona Community from *Iona Abbey Worship Book*, published by Wild Goose Publications, Iona Community Unit 16, Six Harmony Row, Glasgow, Scotland.

Appendix 2

Weaving a Life Story by Carson O. Mouser

Long ago a people were living in a beautiful valley filled with an abundance of grass, grain, water, and fruit. This people raised cattle for milk, raised sheep for wool, fished in nearby streams and planted crops. Some of the people worked in the fields and streams all day while others cared for the children, wove fabric from wool, baked bread and cooked food for the afternoon and evening meals. At the end of each day, the community gathered by the big bonfire and listened to the wise women and wise men tell the stories of how this people began. Each evening ended with giving thanks to God for the blessings of food, health, abundance, and joy. Then, the people went home to bed.

But, there came a time when some of the people said, "perhaps if we worked more hours each day we will be able to raise more crops and gather a greater catch of fish." So they did. They worked so long and so hard that they didn't have time any longer to come to the bonfire. Soon, the wise women and the wise men were only teaching the few children who still came to the bonfire at night. Soon, no one came to the bonfire, not even the children. Then, the rain no longer fell as much and the beautiful valley began changing. The grass withered into dust. The cattle having nothing to eat grew thinner and thinner. Very few fish were caught in the stream. And, the wise women and the wise men began dying until all of them were gone. As each day dawned, the people wore long, sad frowns while they trod slowly to the fields.

One day the small child Julia asked her father, "Where did the rains go?"

Her father shrugged, "I don't know."

So, Julia went to her mother, "Where did the rains go?" Her mother shrugged. So, Julia went to her grandmother, "Grandmother, where did the rains go?" Her grandmother frowned, closed her eyes and touched a wrinkled finger to her head and said, "I seem to remember long ago when I was very, very, very young we would gather around the great bonfire and the wise woman would tell us always to say 'thank you, God' as our grandmothers and grandfathers did every day so long ago."

"But, why?" Julia asked. Her grandmother shrugged. The next morning Julia arose early and ran out of her home and shouted, "Thank you God!" Nothing happened. The next day Julia arose early and ran out of her house and shouted, "Thank you, God!" Nothing happened. A third day Julia arose early and ran out of her house and shouted, "Thank you, God!" Nothing happened. Until, a few drops of rain like snapping fingers began to drop slowly, slowly then faster and faster until lightning and thunder rolled across the sky like a tidal wave of sound and rain. Then Julia shouted with all the people, "Thank you, God!"

In the days that followed the rains, the grass grew green and lush, the cattle grew fatter and the water flowed rapidly down the stream. Each evening the people of the valley gathered at the great bonfire and the wise woman told the story of the day God sent them rain and life.

I tell this story because it tells what happens when a people forget or lose their life story. The life story that describes the way the community came to be, who they are, and why they are a people. When a people or a community have lost their life story, they lose not only their history, but they also lose their identity, and by losing their identity they lose the meaning and purpose for their lives. In my experience of serving congregations and through listening to other people's stories of their communities of faith, I am struck by how often congregations who are in transition have lost their life story and simply wander through the wilderness of their lives without direction and, more importantly, without the health, vitality, or joy of being with God. I have come to firmly believe that the key for congregational transformation resides in reclaiming the biblical narrative as the congregational life story, since within that life story is woven the images and the meaning laden worship acts that foster a congregation's identity leading to the meaning and purpose of their life.

I think in part, Paul is writing his first letter to the house churches in Thessalonica as a way to guide them to find the story of their life as followers of Christ within the longer story of the "people of God" and in doing so is guiding them to comprehend that in that story is where their identity rests as well as the meaning and purpose for this life that is their new reality. Where this intention is most clear comes in his ethical exhortations of 1 Thessalonians 4:1-12.

"Finally, brothers and sisters, we instructed you how to live in order to please God. Now we ask you and urge you in the Lord Jesus to do this more and more." (NIV)

While we do not have sufficient information to tell exactly what previous instructions Paul had given to the Thessalonians, if we read closely the verses that follow I think we can come to an informed conclusion.

First, the Greek word translated "live" is peripatei/n meaning in its basic sense to physically walk, however it also can mean in the figurative sense how one conducts one's life or how one behaves or comport one's self within the community. Paul means the latter, since this is a common use of the word by Paul. Secondly, Paul will come back to this in 4:12 when he suggests the way the Thessalonians live their daily life will have a consequence for how others in the community of Thessalonica will think about them and respond to them.

The movement from the exhortation to live their lives as they were instructed previously to words encouraging them to live in a particular way comes in 4:3-11. In these verses Paul tells the Thessalonians:

"For this is the will of God, your sanctification: that you abstain from fornication;

that each one of you know how to control your own body in holiness and honor, not with lustful passion, like the Gentiles who do not know God; that no one wrong or exploit a brother or sister in this matter, because the Lord is an avenger in all these things, just as we have already told you beforehand and solemnly warned you. For God did not call us to impurity but in holiness. Therefore, whoever rejects this rejects not human authority but God, who also gives his Holy Spirit to you. Now concerning love of the brothers and sisters, you do not need to have anyone write to you, for you yourselves have been taught by God to love one another; and indeed you do love all the brothers and sisters throughout Macedonia. But we urge you, beloved, to do so more and more, to aspire to live quietly, to mind your own affairs, and to work with your hands, as we directed you."

The key in these verses is sanctification, which in the Greek is a`giasmo.j meaning to be dedicated or reserved for God and for God's service. Thus, the Thessalonians are to live in the way that pleases God because they have been dedicated to God for the purpose of serving God by the death and resurrection of Jesus Christ, in whose name and authority Paul and his colleagues have taught them. Therefore, they are to be distant from pornei,aj(or fornication. However, I think it is important to recognize that translating this solely as sexual immorality as though Paul's chief concern was the sexual behavior of the Thessalonians may be limiting and confusing Paul's deeper meaning. In the Septuagint pornei,aj(is also used to indicate adultery and unfaithfulness either to a wife or to God. While space is limited here to fully discuss the issue, there is enough evidence to suggest much of the reference to adultery in the Hebrew Scriptures is much more about unfaithfulness to God and idolatry than it is to only the narrower issue of sexual immorality. This is particularly true in the prophetic texts. For example, Jeremiah 3:9, "Because she (Judah) took her whoredom so lightly, she polluted the land, committing adultery with stone and tree."

So, it is possible, and more likely, given the connection of this verse to the ones preceding and following it that Paul means unfaithfulness to God and idolatry than only sexual immorality. Having said that, I do think this is a pivot passage that allows Paul to move from his focus on the Thessalonians relationship with God to the relationships within the community of believers because it does carry with it the connotation of adultery or improper sexual behavior. Thus, Paul can move from unfaithfulness to God to unfaithfulness to one's spouse then move to unfaithfulness to other members of the community by exhorting the Thessalonians:

"that each one of you know how to control your own body in holiness and honor, not with lustful passion, like the Gentiles who do not know God; that no one wrong or exploit a brother or sister in this matter, because the Lord is an avenger in all these things, just as we have already told you beforehand and solemnly warned you."

Paul links together the people exercising self-control and their relationship with God as a way to say that controlling one's body and lustful passions is not done to show how morally superior one is to their neighbors, rather it is the way one expresses their consecration to God and concretely demonstrates the value placed upon them by God through the grace God gives them as a gift by the cross of Jesus Christ. Essentially, Paul is telling them that their behavior reflects upon their relationship with God and what God has done for them. In addition, the way they live distinguishes them from those around them who do not trust God and who are not in a relationship with God. Paul emphasizes this in the next verse by reiterating it in another way, "For God did not call us to impurity but in holiness."

The boundary lines have been drawn around this community by God's call through Christ and they are to live in the particular way Paul has taught them to live, so that they please God. Failure to do so is not a rejection of Paul or the other apostles; rather it is a rejection of God, who by the Holy Spirit empowers the Thessalonians to live in this way. Once again, Paul has made it clear they are not their own independent, self-sufficient persons able to do whatever it is they want to do either through their will, their knowledge, or their own power.

This marks the transition to the final four verses 9-12, which seem at first to be a bit strange. At least one commentator has likened it to an airplane engine revving up, but never taking off. (Gaventa: 56) I suspect it may be more the case that Paul is transitioning from one portion of his ethical instruction before starting a new set of exhortations in the verses that follow. Thus, his instruction to brotherly love highlights the familial language he has been using throughout his letter, and will continue to employ in the exhortations that follow, by calling the Thessalonians avdelfou.j, which can mean simply brothers, fellow countrymen, or fellow Christians. The familial language and image of the house churches as family is further employed by the use of filadelfi,aj suggesting a familial love each person will have for the others within the community and it is paired with the statement that they know how to love this way because God has taught them to love with love that is self-giving and concerned for the well-being of others. Paul will be more explicit in 5:12-15 about what this might look like among them, but he includes it here to underline that the basis for how they treat one another is by loving each other the way one does a family member and this love is anchored in God's self-giving love, which God has taught them through the cross and resurrection of Jesus Christ.

Paul ends this section of his letter with the instruction to lead a quiet life, to mind their own business and to work with their hands, so that their daily life might win them the respect of their neighbors.

In this final instruction, Paul seems to be telling the Thessalonians to withdraw from the world of politics and public life like many other philosophers of the day instructed their followers to do, and to focus upon doing manual labor that will supply them with the means to provide food, shelter, and clothing and so keep the community intact, however a closer reading suggests that Paul was instructing them to live differently than those people who adopt new philosophies then leave their occupations, becoming either idle or standing in the market place telling everyone within earshot the short comings of their lives while asking for handouts of food, shelter, and clothing. Paul's point is that when other people see how industrious the Thessalonian Christians are, how quiet and how they mind their own business, then those other people will respect them. It is also worth noting that the Thessalonians are not only to be an example to all the people living in Thessalonica, but are an example for the other house churches in Macedonia as well.

This leads me to the point, I believe, Paul is making in his letter. He is calling the Thessalonian Christians to recognize that their lives have been changed by the actions God has taken in the death and resurrection of Jesus Christ and by God calling them and choosing them to be a community, whose life together is defined by God's grace in Jesus Christ that brings them into Christ's family in the kingdom of God. They are now part of "the people of God" and their life together needs to visibly reflect that change.

Paul needs to do this, I think, since most, if not all, the members of the Thessalonian churches were Gentiles and by responding to God's call through Paul's proclamation of the gospel they will have given up their past, including their life story. (Gaventa, 3) To underscore the importance of what the Gentiles gave up it is helpful to speak briefly about the city and culture of Thessalonica.

First, it was a city founded in Macedonia by Alexander in 316 BCE, named for his half-sister Thessaloniki, and is situated on northern coast of the Thracian Sea. As a port city it became increasingly important as a gateway center of commercial and cultic activity for Rome that took over the city in 167 BCE not only because it is a port city, but also because it is located on the Via Egnetia, which was constructed by Rome in 130 BCE, making it easier for travelers and traders to come through the city either from Asia or from Rome. Like other cities of the time there were several indigenous Macedonian cults like those of Cabirus and Dionysus as well as foreign cults like Isis, Serapis and the Roman imperial cult. The Thessalonians actively cultivated the beneficence of the Romans, the result of this was that it was granted the status of a free city which meant they had an independent government. The loyalty shown to Augustus is apparent with numerous statutes honoring him and worshipping him as a god. (Smith: 675-678)

This means that when the Thessalonians converted to following Christ and glorifying Christ, they ran head on into conflict with neighbors and family members who did not convert. Such talk could be considered at best politically charged and at the worst subversive and likely to cause problems for the city, since Rome would not tolerate any subversion of Roman authority and power. Thus, the Thessalonian house churches would be in opposition to the imperial Roman religion of Pax Romana; particularly, when Paul is preaching the inauguration of a new age with Christ's death and resurrection as part of God's transformation of the world. Anyone supporting Jesus, as their benefactor would be seen as trying to weaken support for the Romans, who had brought tangible benefits to the city. As Alan Segal states, "Like the Jews and unlike the many clubs and associations that were part of the civic life of the Hellenistic world, the Christians were exclusive in the sense that no truly committed gentile Christian could maintain cult membership. Thus Christianity was subversive to the basic religious institutions of gentile society." (164; Smith: 678)

While the political ramifications of conversion would certainly have been part of the conflict the house churches of Thessalonica experienced, I suspect the major factor was the conflict that would have erupted within their families. Families were the primary social and economic group in the city. The household was the primary place of socialization into the community where the person learned language, cultural traditions, acceptable behaviors and the consequences of deviating from those behaviors, religious traditions. In addition, relationships within the family defined each person within the family according to their status, power, and work as well as how these family relationships were mirrored within the larger society of the city and beyond the city. Thus, the family gave each person within it identity, meaning, purpose and a life story to live.

Disconnecting from one's family as Gentile converts would have done created reverberations throughout families, since it would have meant the dissolution of familial ties and in some ways, I suspect, created anxiety about the dissolution of the family itself and perhaps the community at large. Again, what happens to the family mirrors what happens to the society. Thus, conflict would have been intense as is suggested by Abraham Malherbe, who has written that people who converted to new religious or philosophical traditions experienced verbal abuse, social dislocation and public criticism. A review of the ancient Mediterranean literature from Philo, Josephus, Juvenal, and Tacitus reveals this when speaking about converts to Judaism, "those who renounce their ancestral traditions and convert to Judaism are taught at the outset to 'despise the gods, to disown their country, and to regard their parents, children, and brothers as of little account." (Still: 231)

Therefore, the Thessalonians who have converted to following Jesus Christ will have experienced severe dislocation and disorientation. Their old ways of being oriented and anchored in the world are gone. Thus through his letter, Paul is guiding them to re-orient their lives. Now, they have a new family within a new community with a new set of relationships that form a new set of kinship ties and relationships extending beyond the family of the house church to all the house churches of Thessalonica and into the larger world of Macedonia and the world. Paul's use of familial language and metaphors is not simply a way to communicate this new reality using images the Thessalonians would have understood. He uses them because they really are a new community whose basis for relationship is the household that has come into existence by God gathering them together as a community following Jesus Christ.

Yet, Paul is also guiding them to comprehend that this new family and community comes with a new reality. They will live differently as this new community. All the old ways of living and orienting themselves to the world are gone. They have a new life orientation and this new life orientation is centered upon God and God's actions for them in Christ and the working of the Holy Spirit among and within them. This new life orientation also leads them to a new life story wherein they have a new identity with a new purpose and meaning for their lives. They are no longer Thessalonians, now they are "the people of God."

Essentially, Paul is speaking about the transformation God inaugurates in Jesus Christ's death and resurrection. It is at this juncture that Gordon Lathrop is helpful to guide us in comprehending what this transformation might be about. Lathrop points to the transformation that happens through Jesus Christ in his discussion of Baptism and the Lord's Supper and specifically in the transformation of water and bread.

As Lathrop points out, Christian baptism is not created out of nothing, but has its beginnings in the bathing practices and the meaning of such practices within Judaism and in the Hellenistic culture that permeated the First Century Mediterranean basin. Bathing rituals for purification were part of Israel from early in its history as is evident in Leviticus 8:6 and 14, Exodus 40:12, and Numbers 19:13. Josephus confirms this with reports of his own teacher Bannus who," lived in the desert, wore clothing supplied from trees and washed many times in cold water both day and night for purification" and Josephus' reports of the repeated full body washings of the Essenes before the common meal, as part of the process of joining the community, washing after contact with strangers, and washing before or instead of offering sacrifices (169-170). Added to this is the list of various other people who are identified, according to Lathrop, "by their accent on repeated and central washings: the daily baptizers, the Masbotheans, the Sabeans, the Banaim, and the morning bathers" (171). John the Baptist's baptism recorded in each of the four gospels would also be included in the list of daily baptizers. While these various baths may not derive from a common ancestor, one thing they do have in common is water and meaning. Whether the bath was a ritual washing before a meal or after an event that made them "ritually impure" the bath once completed indicated some kind of change had taken place making the person "pure" and able to participate in the community activities of meals, worship, etc.

Certainly, this was true for the baptism John performed, since it was part of the preparation for the coming of the Day of the Lord when God would pour out truth and spirit over the people. John's baptism took place in public with the added significance of the water John used. Taking place in the Jordan River, John's baptism drew the crowds coming to him out to the wilderness. The place where the people would re-live the Exodus and the Exile and the Restoration stories. The paradigmatic Exodus experience had two accounts with water; the first is the parting of the Red Sea marking the finality of the Hebrew's escape from slavery to freedom and the second is the wading through the Jordan River to enter into the land God promised them through Abraham, Isaac, and Jacob. The Exile likewise had two water accounts; the first is the people being led off into slavery by the Babylonians through the Jordan as they left the land and the second being their restoration to the land by crossing through the Jordan River.

So, it is not insignificant that John chooses to do his baptism in the Jordan River as the act of repentant preparation of a people who are living in a time of chaos in anticipation of God's washing the people clean promised through the prophets Isaiah 4:2-6 and Ezekiel 36:24-48. John is pointing to God's actions that are central and imminent.

Yet, the moment Jesus steps into the water of the Jordan River according to the gospel accounts of his baptism by John, baptism is transformed. As Lathrop states it, "Jesus is the coming Mighty One; his baptism transforms Baptism itself, making it the very presence of God (the voice and the dove); and henceforth Baptism in him is the outpouring of the Holy Spirit, the dawning of the day of God, one's beginning to hear the voice of God and the joining of the holy assembly before the coming God." Added to this is the deeper meaning of baptism as a sign of the transformative cross and tomb that is carried out through the gospels when water becomes significant in the story whether it is the Samaritan woman at the well, the sick man at the pool of Siloam, the washing of the blind man's eyes, the water turned to wine at Cana, or the foot washing in the upper room. According to Lathrop, in each of these the water is Jesus, who pours out his life through his death on the cross and who becomes the living water in his resurrection. Thus, when the person goes down under the water they are united in Jesus' death and when they come out they are united in Jesus' resurrection.

For Christians, ordinary water is transformed not only when it is placed in the baptismal font or immersion pool, but is transformed in all the places where water might be whether wells, oceans, rivers, lakes or streams to be a sign pointing to the life and grace of God in Jesus Christ, since all water may be used for baptism.

The same thing can be said of bread, particularly bread eaten at meals. Lathrop points out that there was a Mediterranean way of eating meals and many of these particular practices occurred at Jewish meals during the First Century. However, Jewish meal practice included a meaning not found at Gentile meal practices. Each meal included a prayer of thanksgiving and supplication with the recognition that the food is eaten with thanksgiving to God for what God has done for the family gathered around the meal table and is eaten before God who is present at the meal. Bread takes on a particular importance as a reminder recalling the bread eaten at Abraham and Gideon's meals as well as recalling the bread of the Exodus. It is important, I think, to realize that meals and bread were significant symbols in the life of the Jewish family and community pointing them to the paradigmatic events of the Exodus, not only for the bread they ate leaving Egypt, but also the bread like manna of the wilderness. It is significant that Passover is celebrated around a meal table as a way not so much to recall events, but to re-live those events as though they happened to each person around the table. Around the Passover table, the food and the prayers and the readings of scripture tell the story about God's saving act and the reconstitution of the people as God's people and a reinsertion of those around the table into the faith of Israel, according to Lathrop, (187).

Like he did with baptism, Jesus comes eating meals around tables with those people considered to be sinners and outcast and transforms meals and bread. He rejects, as Lathrop points out, the rules of purity intended to accentuate the identity of the very people the meal was meant to constitute and welcomes all who sit at table with him to be part of the people of God and as an enactment of the life-giving participation in God's kingdom. However, like the instances of water, the meals Jesus shares with others is given a deeper meaning when he sits down to eat with his disciples one last meal and takes bread and breaks it telling his disciples the broken bread is his body that is broken for them. Now, the bread is Jesus and Jesus is the bread of life. Next, Jesus takes wine and pours it into a cup telling his disciples it is his blood shed for the forgiveness of sins and that the cup he offers them is a new covenant in him, who is broken and poured out. His breaks his body and pours out his life, so all who drink of the cup and eat the bread have life. The next meal Jesus will share, according to Luke at least, is at a table in the Emmaus Inn. Here, Jesus will act as host to two disciples, by breaking bread and handing it to them as their eyes are opened to the reality of the Risen Christ.

For Christians, bread and wine are thus transformed as are meals shared around table because now all of our meals are eaten with the Crucified and Risen One. All of the wine we drink and all of the bread we eat are signs for us to remember, relive and re-experience, as though it is happening for the first time, Christ's body being broken and his life being poured out, so we might receive life by God's grace through the cross and resurrection of Jesus Christ and take our place within the people of God.

Just as God in Jesus Christ transforms meals, baptism, water, wine and bread, so too does God in Jesus Christ transform ordinary people into being the people of God. This is particularly true for the Thessalonians in the house churches to whom Paul is writing his letter and I think Paul was well aware of it.

Significantly, as I read 4:1-12, I was struck by the implicit way Paul was placing the Thessalonians within the continuity of the long story of Israel by the way he first spoke about their relationship with God and what God was doing with and for them. Then, secondly he pivots to their relationship with each other, then he again pivots to their purpose of being an example not only for the Macedonian churches, but also for those living around them, who did not know God by not being a threat or a disruptive element in the community, but instead being a quiet blessing within the community. I do not think Paul forms his admonition or instruction by accident, rather I think he is consciously placing them within the context of the Exodus and Sinai, since the form he uses and even his words reflect back to the covenant of ten words given at Sinai and repeated in Leviticus 19:1-18.

The covenant of ten words as it begins in Exodus 20 with God instructing the people about the way they are to live first by emphasizing, the Lord alone is their God and they shall not worship idols or other gods, but worship God solely and keeping the Sabbath holy; then God continues by outlining the relationship between the people of the community which includes being faithful to spouses and not coveting another persons' possessions. Leviticus 19:1-18 begins with a reiteration of God's instructions that because God is holy the people also are to be holy followed by the prescriptive teaching of the ten commands along with teaching about not causing neighbors to stumble, the way justice is to be practiced within the community, then ending with the admonition to love their neighbor as they love themselves.

In addition, the promise God makes to Abraham is not only for progeny and land, but the purpose for Abraham and his having numerous children is so that they will be God's blessing to the world. Likewise, Moses in Deuteronomy 4 as part of his recitation of Exodus history admonishes the Hebrews to observe all that God has commanded Moses to teach them, "for this will show your wisdom and understanding to the nations, who will hear about these decrees and say, 'Surely, this great nation is a wise and discerning people. What other nation is so great as to have their gods so near them the way the Lord our God is near us…"

The themes Paul is teaching the Thessalonians- live a way pleasing to God, holiness of the people, faithfulness to God, faithfulness to each other, loving each other, God's teaching of the people, and being the example of wisdom to other people -match very well with the ten words of the covenant given at Sinai and repeated in Leviticus. Paul is firmly, if not explicitly, calling the Thessalonians to see their identity and the meaning and purpose for the lives in continuity and in solidarity with Israel as the "people of God."

As an image the "people of God" does provide a rich and deep sense of identity that spans time and place and is connected with God's saving action and promises of life that are fulfilled in Jesus Christ. The richness of this image, as Minear points out, is its focus not on a gathering of individual persons as an aggregate number, but as a way to speak about a particular people through whom the individual person is defined. The community's existence determines the existence and the identity of the person. When a person makes a shift from belonging to one people to belonging to another people, a change in self-understanding and status is involved. Additionally, identifying an assembly of people as "the people of God" sets them over and against other people because the "people of God" are those people God alone has created for God's purpose.

The focus is "first God and God's purposes, then the emergence of this people as a manifestation of God's purpose. The accent must be allowed to fall on God who creates society as his people by his choice of them." (Minear: 69) "The people of God" then are dependent upon God's gracious and faithful actions for their creation, their purpose for being, their continuing life, and their survival. The only reason they are a people is because of what God does, not what they do. Their actions are a response to what God has already done.

Minear is very helpful to complete this picture through the concrete images of Israel, including chosen race, the twelve tribes, the patriarchs, and especially the exodus. Each of these images brings to mind one overarching image of the people God by speaking about the solidarity of the Christian communities, like the Thessalonians, with the Jewish community, so that there is not two "people of God" as if somehow the Christians supplanted the Jewish community out of being "the people of God." Thus, Israel speaks about the unity and oneness of the people of God, as measured, according to Minear, qualitatively by God's mercy in the cross of Christ. Israel, then is, the people who receive the gospel and through whom God's mission or intention for the world is accomplished and is the same Israel who received promises from God and whose promises were fulfilled in Jesus Christ. "Chosen race" does not speak about ethnicity, rather it identifies all the people God has chosen or elected to be God's people Israel with the emphasis upon God's choosing and not biological genealogy. This does lead nicely into the image of the twelve tribes whose identity stems from the patriarchs, who were their living representatives. It is fairly easy then to identify the twelve disciples not only with the twelve tribes, but also as being identical to the patriarchs because the God of the apostolic community is identical with the God of the fathers. Also, within the twelve tribes once again the oneness, the fullness, and the wholeness of the people of God are affirmed such that there is a single inclusive promise and a single inclusive hope. (Minear: 73)

Finally, the Exodus image draws Christians into "the people of God" through the experience of being set free and walking through a wilderness where learning to trust God and being dependent upon God for life is the primary people-creating paradigm with that trust and dependency being expressed with words of thanksgiving and lives of praise according to the way God teaches a people to live.

The importance of Paul's teaching the Thessalonians to find their new identity, their meaning and purpose, and their life story within the long continuity and solidarity of the people of God coupled with Lathrop's use of liturgy and narrative and Minear's use of image is that it provides a way for guiding contemporary congregations who are in transition to reclaim the biblical narrative as their life story for transformation into being healthy and vital communities of grace and life.

Many congregations caught up in transition--whether it is the transition of the interim time between permanent pastors, the transition from a large membership congregation to a small membership congregation, or the transition of a congregation caught in the overwhelming economic and social changes of urban America--have lost the biblical narrative that is the story of all of life and in losing that encompassing narrative they no longer find their own personal life stories placed within any one encompassing narrative. Rather, they attempt to live within a number of competing narratives (American citizen, occupation, consumerism, etc) none of which includes who they are fully and none of which give meaning or purpose for their lives, and none that have the ability to nurture and sustain life. So, they feel as if they are looking through a very dark kaleidoscope and seeing their life distorted into oddly shaped fragments that are constantly shifting without rhyme or reason causing them to be so disoriented that nothing makes sense any longer. Having lost the encompassing narrative-the story of all of life-they have, also, lost their identity and have lost the meaningfulness and the purposefulness for their lives flowing from that identity.

My reason for firmly believing that reclaiming the biblical narrative as life story can be transformative for congregations comes from my own penchant for writing and telling stories, acting in plays, the way I have taught Bible stories to children by having them become persons in the stories then act out the stories by becoming the biblical person so well that they are able to answer questions about themselves as though they really were that person. In addition, my reading and experience about the importance of stories for creating identity and comprehending meaning for life, particularly the work of Stanley Hauerwas in *A Community of Character*, George Stroup, and John Drane.

As George Stroup describes it:

"The crucial theological issue of our day is not whether the Christian community can find acceptance and understanding in other religious communities. On the contrary the question is whether the church can rediscover the sense in which it stands in and lives out of a tradition, reinterpret that tradition so that it is intelligible in the contemporary world, and offer a clear description of Christian faith, which makes it relevant to the urgent questions, and issues of modern society.

In sum, the present crisis in the church is a deep-seated confusion about Christian identity." (24)

This confusion comes largely from biblical illiteracy becoming so dominate in many congregations as well as the church becoming so enmeshed within modernity that the church has lost the biblical narrative that is essential to a community's self-understanding and, as Hauerwas points out, losing this narrative impacts and influences their ability to be a community, let alone be the community Christ calls into being (9-35).

John Drane affirms this in *The McDonaldization of the Church*, saying, "Story is central to the contemporary quest for meaning, in much the same way as abstract analysis was central to the outlook of modernity" (156). I would hasten to add that story has always been foundationally important for human communities. We are always telling stories about our lives that include our relationships, the places we have been, who our parents and grandparents are, the history of our families and the connections that seem to cross from one family to another and from one community to another as well as how we fit into the context of the world. Embedded within our stories are the clues to our identity, how we comprehend the workings of the world, and the meaning and purpose for our lives (155-168).

Take for example, the opening verses of Jeremiah 1:1-5:

"The words of Jeremiah son of Hilkiah, of the priests who were in Anathoth in the land of Benjamin, to whom the word of the Lord came in the days of the King Josiah son of Amon of Judah in the 13th year of his reign. It came also in the days of King Jehoiakim son of Josiah of Judah, and until the end of the 11th year of King Zedekiah son of Josiah of Judah, until captivity of Jerusalem in the fifth month. Now the word of the Lord came to me saying, "Before I formed you in the womb I knew you, and before you were born I consecrated you; I appointed you a prophet to the nations."

Here in this brief passage we learn a great deal about Jeremiah. We know the essential relationships of his life. First is God's relationship with Jeremiah that begins in his mother's womb and second is his relationship with his family in Anathoth, who are priests. Indeed, we find out his father's name and his tribe. We also learn that he was writing before and until Jerusalem was captured and the people sent into exile, so we have an historical time when he lived. We have the beginnings of a relationship with this prophet who lived about 2,700 years ago. If we read further, we will learn more about him and the depth and characteristics of the relationship he has with God and his community. All of this we gleaned from just a small portion of his life story.

While I had learned years ago the connection between story, identity and purpose and meaning for life, first intuitively as a child creating my own worlds and inhabiting them as different people in my imagination then as a student and practitioner of story, I was struck by it again in Douglas Coupland's *Polaroids from the Dead*, as part of the argument Drane makes that people are searching for a metanarrative that will encompass their lives in such a way that they will have the ability to navigate through the turbulent waters of the present age when life seems to be fragmented, disjointed, and meaningless (169-177).

Particularly, I suspect people are searching for a metanarrative that includes their own life story within it not as a propositional story that is offered as one which people may adapt themselves into, rather as the story of life that already contains their life experiences, the meaning of those experiences for life, and a context for discerning their identity and what is, as a theology professor once said, "the really real."

What I am suggesting is weaving together three connecting stories-God's story, Bible stories, and personal stories-such that they become not three distinct stories, but threads woven into the tapestry of one, holistic story which is told both in the testimony of the Bible and in the testimony of people's present experiences with God and with one another as an intensely relational reality. The value of doing this is that weaving this one holistic story will build community by people's willingness to be vulnerable with others, respecting and cherishing the vulnerability of others, and being a place of healing, health, vitality, compassion, hope, learning, and a community where, as Martin Luther King Jr. often said, "your concerns are my concerns and where I cannot fully be all that I am to be until you are fully who you are to be."

Having said all of this, it is important to recognize that reclaiming the narrative is not simply a matter of a better Bible study or a different way of studying the Bible because those in and of themselves would not engage the many people in congregations in the deep-seated change of heart that transformation is about, since most of the people have participated in or have led such study groups in the past. Therefore, what is needed is a new approach that asks different questions, demands different answers, and is counter-intuitive to the narratives congregations have been living within.

Thus, a year and a half ago I began my service to the congregation of First Presbyterian Church, Gloversville by designing a process for transformation that begins with a series of workshops designed to begin reclaiming the biblical narrative by reclaiming the language of orientation, lament and re-orientation leading to a series of workshops designed to speak to transformation by discovering our life stories within the biblical narrative. These workshops led to creation of a one sentence identity statement that everyone in the congregation knows and can say aloud. From this identity statement we asked the question, "if this is who we say we are then what are we to do to make that concrete and visible within the congregation and the community?" The question was answered by looking at our worship liturgy and by beginning four new ministries to the community all of which seek to end the systemic causes of poverty. I should note these ministries came from the congregation and not from me.

Now, as we continue to seek ways to reclaim the biblical narrative and weave our lives into it, I can begin incorporating Minear's work with images as a guide to move through Scripture, somewhat the way I did earlier in this paper, to see how the images take shape and find those images that will inform our identity and our way being community as well as find those particular images that draw people into the one holistic narrative. In addition, I find Lathrop's work with Jesus transforming the ordinary to be particularly useful and I will be using his focus on how Jesus transforms the ordinary into the sacred as part of our Lenten worship and education praxis this year to speak more clearly about being the transformed assembly of "the people of God."

About the Author
Rev. Dr. Carson O. Mouser

I am one of the rarities of the last century, a native Californian. I was born in a Los Angeles County hospital and my first home was a tent on a beach before my family moved to the San Francisco Bay area where I lived until I entered the United States Air Force in 1969. Throughout my childhood, my family lived what might best be described as a nomadic life, since we moved every year and a half from community to community and I rarely spent more than a year and a half in any school until high school. Thus, I am very comfortable with change and is probably the reason my doctoral work was about change and congregational responses to change.

When I was 15 I was hired to write for a local weekly newspaper beginning a 15-year career as a reporter, editor, and free-lance feature writer for newspapers and magazines. Also, I have worked in public relations and marketing for Ohlone Community College, the Mental Health Association of Santa Clara County, and a variety of non-profit organizations. My work experience in journalism is complimented by an A.A. degree in Liberal Studies with a major in Journalism from Ohlone College in 1975 and a Bachelor of Arts degree in Journalism and U.S. History from San Jose State University in 1976. While at Ohlone College I was editor of the college newspaper and was awarded the Journalism Department Award and received a Third Place for Editorials in a statewide competition of Community College Newspapers. In addition, I have graduate coursework in both business administration and United States economic history as well as course work in insurance underwriting, group health insurance and pension analysis.

Along with a 15-year career in journalism, I have experience in the United States Air Force, retail store management and 13 years in the insurance industry.

During the final years of my insurance career, I felt God pulling at my heart and sensed a call to ministry as a Minister of Word and Sacrament in the Presbyterian Church (U.S.A.), which my wife had been encouraging me to pursue for many years. I had been a member of the First Presbyterian Church, Pittsford where I served as a Sunday school teacher, member of the Christian Education Committee and on the Board of Deacons. At First Presbyterian, Pittsford my journey of faith was re-awakened, nourished and encouraged to a greater depth, and my call was affirmed by both Rev. Baron Ashfield and Rev. Dr. Earl Johnson. While at seminary I served as a seminary intern at Twelve Corners Presbyterian Church and following graduation continued to serve Twelve Corners as the first Director of Educational Ministries until my ordination to the Ministry of Word and Sacrament in 1998. In addition, I served the Presbytery of Genesee Valley on its Youth Committee during my time with Twelve Corners as well as participating in Youth Conferences at Montreat Conference Center as a small group leader. I have served four congregations as pastor and head of staff as well as serving as a Campus Pastor at Paul Smith's College and have served three congregations as an intentional interim minister using all of the skills and experiences garnered in all of my previous vocational work and all the study and research I have done over the last thirty- five years. I have a Master of Divinity degree from Colgate Rochester Crozer Divinity School with a specialization in Biblical Studies and a Doctor of Ministry degree from Columbia Theological Seminary, Decatur, GA. My doctoral work focused on congregational transformation through reclaiming the biblical narrative as the call to be the community of Christ within the specialized area of Gospel and Culture.

During my doctoral studies I created a narrative mission study process for congregations in transition to use as a way to express their grief over the changes they have experienced, a way to comprehend a new identity and through a focus on that identity and their passion for particular missions to discern what God is calling them to do both in the context of their local community and their global community. I have used this study process in congregations I have served and it has been the preferred mission study process used in the Albany Presbytery for the last four or five years.

I am married to Tina, who is an RN serving in the outpatient behavioral health clinic at the Canandaigua VA and is a graduate of St. John Fisher College. We have five adult children and six grandchildren. My interests include contemplative prayer, craft brewing beer, photography, hiking the 46 High peaks of the Adirondacks, golf, travel, fiction writing, poetry writing and reading, particularly, economic history, poetry, local history and mystery stories.

One of my favorite quotes comes from Wendell Berry, "When despair for the world grows in me and I wake in the night at the least sound in fear of what my life and my children's lives may be, I go and lie down where the wood drake rests in his beauty on the water, and the great heron feeds. I come down into the peace of wild things who do not tax their lives with forethought of grief. I come into the presence of still water and I feel above me the day blind stars waiting with their light. For a time, I rest in the grace of the world, and am free."

This quote speaks to me about creation relationships, Sabbath rest that relieves anxiousness, and solitude as a key for clarity and the mindfulness of prayer.

Two other quotes speak about the renewing of an authentic spirituality through simplicity and my own inclination as a storyteller to see within scripture a life story for every person and community of faith connecting us to all our ancestors and to all who come after us in the long narrative of God and God's people. The first is "The call to simplicity and freedom for Christians is the call to move from achievement oriented spirituality to a life centered on a shared vision of relatedness, of gentleness, of compassion, of belonging to one another" by Richard Bower and the second is, "I want my life to be a novel, not a short story," by Joan Didion.

End Notes

[1] The Pastor Nominating Committee told me this was the reason several candidates had given for not continuing the call process with them.

[2] Nearly all the reading I have done recently has included a descriptor about post-modernism or post-modernity including the discussion about whether it is one word or two words and one might be preferred over and against the other. In addition, few if any have of the commentators have firm description about what is or is not postmodern, except that there is no one voice offering a simple answer, which may be the most important point to be made about the changes being experienced today. These changes may only be comprehended within the diversity of the conversation partners and their diverse perspectives and questions.

[3] One example of the complexity of these changes is understanding the development of power alliances between nations birthed during the Wars of the Spanish Succession and carried forward in the way the Cold War was fought in client states of the dominant world powers of Russia, United States, Europe, and China from Korea to Vietnam to Cuba, to Bolivia and El Salvador. Further changes in power alliances came about when communism collapsed under the weight of its economic failures, political oppression, and the refusal of people from Poland and East Germany to Czechoslovakia, Yugoslavia, and Hungary to continue living within such repression and collapse and when countries that had been formed by political demarcation were shattered by the rise of ethnic majorities eager to establish nations reflecting their majority, such as when the Serbians created Serbia.

[4] The change in work and the making of goods from small artisan shops to factories and the continued rise in mass production is well documented in many histories of the United States whether dealing with urban mass production or rural mass production of agricultural products. In addition, the rise of rationalized systems for efficiency in manufacture of goods is also well documented in a number of histories that are too numerous to mention specifically here. However, to begin reading further see Melvyn Dubofsky, *Industrialism and the American Worker, 1865–1920*, ed. John Hope Franklin, The AHM American History Series, (Arlington Heights, ILL: AHM Publishing Corp. 1978) and David Brody, *Workers in Industrial America: Essays on the 20th Century Struggle* (New York, NY: Oxford University Press 1980)

[5] The terms transformation, renewal, revitalization and redevelopment are used interchangeably in the literature of congregational change. Therefore, I will only use the term transformation as including all the terms of revitalization, renewal and redevelopment.

[6] Walter Brueggemann offers another way of stating this that I think is very valuable for congregations to hear, though he is referring to ancient Israel, "Israel's narrative is a partisan, polemical narrative. It is concerned to build a counter community--counter to the oppression of Egypt, counter to the seduction of Canaan, counter to every cultural alternative and every imperial pretense. There is nothing in this narrative that will appeal to outsiders who belong to another consensus, or who share a different ethos and participate in another epistemology. To such persons, Israel's narratives are silly, narrow, scandalous, and obscurantist. The narrative form of the Torah intends to nurture insiders who are willing to risk a specific universe of discourse and cast their lot there" (1982:27).

[7] Gordon W. Lathrop in *Holy Things: A Liturgical Theology* (Minneapolis: Fortress Press 1993) offers an in-depth discussion of worship which is valuable for thinking about worship and its meaning for congregations as well as asking questions of those who plan and lead worship that challenge us to think more deeply about centering our worship and our lives in God.

Select Bibliography

Avery, William O. 2000 *Revitalizing Congregations: Refocusing and Healing Through Transitions*. Bethesda, MD: The Alban Institute.

Bandy, Thomas G. 1998*Moving Off the Map: A Field Guide to Changing the Congregation*. Nashville: Abingdon Press.

Barna, George *Without a VISION, the People Perish*. Glendale, CA: Barna Research group, Ltd.

Battin, Barbara and Richard Bell ed. *Seeds of the Spirit: Wisdom of Twentieth Century*. Louisville: Westminster John Knox Press.

Bradt, Kevin, M. SJ 1997*Story as a Way of Knowing*. Kansas City: Sheed & Ward.

Bridges, William *Transitions: Making Sense of Life's Changes*. Philippines: Addison-Wesley Publishing Company, Inc.

Brueggemann, Walter *The Message of the Psalms: A Theological Commentary*. Minneapolis: Augsburg.

Buchanan, David, Louise Fitzgerald, Diane Ketley, Rose Gollop, Jane Louise Jones, Sharon Saint Lamont, Annette Neath and Elaine Whitby 2005" No going back: A review of the literature on sustaining organizational change,"
International Journal of Management Review 7, no. 3:189-205.

Burke, Trevor J. *Family Matters: A Socio-Historical Study of Kinship Metaphors in 1Thessalonians* London: T&T Clark International.

Burnes, Bernard, 2004 "Kurt Lewin and the Planned Approach to Change: A Re-appraisal" *International Journal of Management Review* 41, no 6:977-1002.

Coffey, Ian and Eddie Gibbs 2001*Church Next: Quantum Changes in Christian Ministry*. Downers Grove, IL: Inter-Varsity Press.

Coupland, Douglas 1991*Generation X*. New York: St Martins Press.

1994*Life After God*. New York: Simon & Schuster.

Cousar, Charles B. *A Theology of the Cross: The Death of Jesus in the Pauline Letters*. Minneapolis: Fortress Press.

Craig, Robert H. and Robert C. Worley 1992 *Dry Bones Live: Helping Congregations Discover New Life*. Louisville: Westminster/John Knox Press.

Crites, Stephen 1971" The Narrative Quality of Experience" in *Why Narrative? Readings in Narrative Theology*, pp. 65-88 Stanley Hauerwas and L. Gregory Jones ed. Grand Rapids: William B. Erdmans Publishing Co.

Coles, E. 1989*The Call of Stories*. Boston: Houghton Mifflin.

Detweiler, Craig and Barry Taylor 2003*A Matrix of Meanings: Finding God in Pop Culture*. Grand Rapids: Baker Academic.

Drane, John *Cultural Change and Biblical Faith*. Waynesboro, GA; Paternoster Press.

The McDonaldization of the Church: Consumer Culture and the 2001Church's Future. Macon: Smyth & Helwys Publishing, Inc.

First Presbyterian Church, Gloversville "Annual Meeting of the Congregation and Corporation of First Presbyterian Church, Gloversville" in Session Minutes Jan. 25, 1978. Gloversville, NY. 2005" Annual Meeting of the Congregation and Corporation of First Presbyterian Church, Gloversville" in Session Minutes Jan. 30, 2005. Gloversville, NY.

Grossman, Gail, Mary K. Sellon and Daniel P. Smith 2002 *Redeveloping the Congregation: A How to for Lasting Change.* Bethesda, MD: Alban Institute.

Hannah, William S. "The Narrative: The Centrality of Story to Human Understanding of Self and God. An Exploration into Narrative from Theological, Psychological and Homiletical Perspectives." DMin. diss., Columbia Theological Seminary.

Hauerwas, Stanley 1981 *A Community of Character: Toward a Constructive Christian Social Ethic.* Notre Dame, IN: University of Notre Dame Press.

Heelas, Paul and Linda Woodhead ed. 2005 *The Spiritual Revolution: Why Religion is Giving Way to Spirituality*, Malden, MA: Blackwell Publishing Ltd.

Jodock, Darrell 1981 "Story and Scripture," *Word & World*, 1 no. 2: 28-139.

Kindig, E.S. 1997*Remember the Time*. Downers Grove, IL: InterVarsity Press

Kotter, John P. 1986 *Leading Change*. Boston: Harvard Business School Press.

Kritsonis, Alicia 2004-05 "Comparison of Change Theories" in *International Journal of Scholarly Academic Intellectual Diversity*. vol.8, issue 1pp.1-7

Kubler-Ross, Elisabeth *On Death and Dying: What the Dying Have to Teach Doctors, Nurses, Clergy, and Their Own Families*. New York: MacMillan.

Lathrop, Gordon W. 1993 *Holy Things: A Liturgical Theology*. Minneapolis: Fortress Press. *Holy People: A Liturgical Ecclesiology*. Minneapolis: Augsburg Fortress Press.

Loughlin, Gerard 1996*Telling God's Story: Bible, Church, and Narrative Theology*. Cambridge, Great Britain: Cambridge University Press.

Mehl-Madrona, Lewis, Erik Juhl and Barbara Mainguy 2014 "Results of Transpersonal, Narrative, and Phenomenological Psychotherapy for Psychosis" in *International Journal of Transpersonal Studies* vol. 33 issue 1 pp.57-76

Manning, H. A. 1971*Manning's Gloversville and Johnstown Directory 1971*. Schenectady, NY: H.A. Manning Co.

MacIntyre, Alasdair 1977 "Epistemological Crises, dramatic Narrative, and the Philosophy of Science" in *Why narrative? Readings in Narrative Theology*, pp. 138-157 Grand Rapids: William Erdmans Publishing Company.

1981" Virtue, Unity of a Human Life, and Tradition" in *Why Narrative? Readings in Narrative Theology*, pp. 89-110

Stanley Hauerwas, L. Gregory Jones ed. Grand Rapids: William B. Erdmans Publishing Company.

Minear, Paul S. *Images of the Church in the News Testament.* Louisville: Westminster John Knox Press.

Mitchell, Gary 2013" Selecting the Best Theory to Implement Planned Change" in Nursing *Management.* Vol 20, issue 1 pp. 32-37.

Nicholson, Roger S. *Temporary Shepherds: A Congregational Handbook for Interim Ministry.* Bethesda, MD: Alban Institute, Inc.

Niebuhr, H. Richard 1941 "The Story of Our Life," in Why Narrative? Readings in Narrative Theology, pp. 21-44 Stanley Hauerwas, L. Gregory Jones ed. Grand Rapids: William B. Erdmans Publishing Co.

Rarick, Judith E. "Into the Future: A Process to Begin Redevelopment in the Smaller Congregation." DMin. diss., Columbia Theological Seminary.

Saliers, Don E. "Human Pathos and Divine Ethos" in *Primary Sources of Liturgical Theology: A Reader.* Dwight Vogel, ed. Collegeville, MN: The Liturgical Press.

Sherwood, G 2000 "The Power of Nurse Client Encounters" in *Journal of Holistic Nursing* vol. 18 issue 2 pp 159-175. 2000 "Story: Informing Caring Nursing Practice" in *International Journal of Human Caring* vol.4, issue 2, pp. 5.

Stroup, George W. *The Promise of Narrative Theology: Recovering the Gospel in the Church.* Atlanta: John Knox Press.

Bureau of the Census 2000 "Fact Sheet" in *U.S. Census Bureau Summary File 1 and Summary File 3*, accessed 5 December 2006; available from http://factfinder.census.gov./serlet.html; Internet.

Westeroff John H., III *Living the Faith Community: The Church That Makes Difference.* Minneapolis: Winston Press, Inc.

Willimon, William H. *Shaped by The Bible.* Nashville: Abingdon Press.

Zimmerman, Joyce Ann "Paschal Mystery—Whose Mystery? A Post-Critical Methodological Reinterpretation." in *Primary Sources of Liturgical Theology: A Reader*, pp. 302-312 *Collegeville*, MN: The Liturgical Press.

Carson O. Mouser

www.ingramcontent.com/pod-product-compliance
Lightning Source LLC
Chambersburg PA
CBHW052140110526
44591CB00012B/1802